NOT FORGOTTEN

Published by:

Herstory Global Hub LLC

Email: Stefanie@herstoryglobalhub.com

Website: www.herstoryglobalhub.com

ISBN: **979-8-218-94320-2**

This book is a work of heart, faith, and legacy. All scripture quotations, unless otherwise noted, are taken from the Holy Bible and used with reverence. The views expressed here belong to the author and do not necessarily reflect those of the publisher.

Printed in the United States of America

NOT FORGOTTEN

The Memoir of
REBEKAHANNMCKAY

Dedication

To every child who has ever felt lost, alone
or forgotten in the foster care system.
This story is for you.

May you always remember that your life
is precious, your voice matters,
and your dreams are worth holding onto.

Your circumstances do not define you,
but by the hope, courage, and love of Heavenly Father God.

May you find comfort, belonging, and the unwavering belief
that you are never truly alone.

Table of Contents

INTRODUCTION

There is an epidemic among us. It is passed on from generation to generation. Those who suffer from it are our most precious resource. They are our children. Every hour, children die at the hands of those they trust to protect them. It is a painful and sometimes slow death. It is not always a physical death to the body, but even more tragic, in that it kills the soul. It condemns our children to a hopeless existence. We build prisons for the carriers of this disease, for without love, no life exists in their souls, and they take the lives of others. The disease is child abuse, abandonment, and neglect.

The cure is Love for all children. Their only Hope is salvation, paid long ago, on a cross. Who will tell them of the Father who loved them so much that He sent His only Son? When the Cure of His Love is received at an early age, the developmental process and hope are nurtured. And the disease is less likely to spread to future generations. We cannot say, "they are not our children." As wards of the court, they are now. But they were always God's children... someone didn't have time or didn't know how to show His love. As a result, hopeless and loveless children fill juvenile detention centers and eventually graduate to prisons. Too many youth in the juvenile system today were the children we didn't reach with His love yesterday. Now that you know about this disease and vulnerable victims, you cannot look the other way.

**"Who will be willing to obey the Father
to use you as a vessel to pour out His love
to these children and their families?"**

There is a story of victory I must tell, but first, let me paint a picture. The Columbine tragedy flashes across television screens everywhere. Children are killing each other and themselves. Violence is rampant, even in elementary schools. Increasing numbers of these troubled teenagers seek fulfillment and acceptance in vandalism, crime, and drugs. Streetwise, hardened hearts fill juvenile jails. Many of them, aging out of foster care, have no hope of being adopted or knowing the structure or stability that comes from a family that serves God. We shake our heads and wonder what has happened to the world....to the children. Some look the other way, focusing on their own children and turning a blind eye to those who cry out to us for help. Many are guarding their own trees while the forest burns out of control. As Christians, we diligently defend the unborn, as we should, and yet deny others the nurturing essential to the developmental process so they might truly live. To live without love is death to the soul... not just living death, but an eternal one. God wants to pour His love through us into the lives of His children.

So, now let me share another visual with you. Imagine you are a young boy or girl...seven or eight years old, moved from home to home, shelter to shelter, feeling unwanted and unloved by even your own parents. How will you survive? Does your heart become hardened? Do you grow up not knowing the value of life, not even your own? Who is supposed to teach them the ways they should go, so that when they are older, they will not part from it? Who will teach them what love is? The word of God says Without love, we have nothing.... Why are the children hopeless? Because they do not know a Supernatural Love that only comes from God.

> *Pure and undefiled religion before God and the Father is this: to visit orphans and widows in their trouble, and to keep oneself unspotted from the world.*
> *James 1:27*

Now I will tell you a story of a child's heart that was not allowed to harden by the Grace and Mercy of God through Faith in Jesus, how Heavenly Father God heard my heart cries and kept me in the midst of immense loss!

"I will share how God has not forgotten any child.
And I will tell of the unfailing love
of a Heavenly Father,"

How God worked through people and circumstances. He used a stranger with a willing heart, an extra room to spare, and most importantly, the love of Jesus to share. It was a moment's touch that lasts a lifetime. I am where I am and who I am, and able to share His love with others because someone like you gave the most incredible gift of love.

WHERE ARE THE CHILDREN?

By Rebekah McKay, 1997

Where is the newborn infant thrown away?
Whose cries are never heard?

Where is the young girl who, out of fear, never says a word.
Where is the troubled teen? Who feels forgotten and alone?
Where is the very young mother unable to give,
a love she's never known.

I speak for the children, unable to speak for themselves,
for the children who cry out in vain.

For the children lost in a system that offers safety,
but lacks nurturing, essential to their developmental process,
essential to their existence. For children who blame
themselves for everything tragic in their lives.

For children who feel all alone,
in a big world of new places and strangers.

For the children who are afraid of tomorrow.
For the children lost in a system and forgotten.
For the children who grow up unloved and unable to love
others. For the children who cry to sleep at night.
For children who can no longer cry
whose hearts have turned to stone.

For the children who are shuffled like a deck of cards
from place to place in their best interests.

For the children who have no choice in their lives.

I do not speak on behalf of foster parents,
who, in a short amount of time, can redirect a child's life.

I do not speak on behalf of the child welfare system
that fails a child more often than not,
or the dedicated social workers' concerns that go
unrewarded and underfunded.

I speak for the children who cannot speak
for themselves unable to help themselves.

That's our job.... The Church.

Chapter 1

A Mother's Love

My father, Larry Wayne McKay, and my mother, Martha Ann, were married when she was just 16. My father was a preacher; my mother was a preacher's wife. At 17, my mother gave birth to James Michael, the firstborn son, on October 14, 1959. Joel Stephen, her second son, was born on January 29, 1961.

I was born on January 12, 1962. My father opened his Bible (as was his custom for naming all his children) upon my birth and called me Rebekah Ann. On May 6, 1963, my brother John David was born. Shortly after my parents' divorce, my father married Deanna. She was living as a nun in St Teresa's Convent when she met my father.

The sisters (nuns) had raised her since her mother died during childbirth of her younger brother. Soon after marriage to my father, they had my brother Joseph McKay March 23, 1964, my brother Timothy Andrew on June 15, 1965.

Meanwhile, my mother met Sidney Laza at the hospital where she worked. They were married, and my brother, Sidney Laza Jr., was born on June 17, 1965. It seemed like a time of new beginnings for both my father and my mother, but it was not to be. The tragedies of my life began early. On August 11, 1965, our mother was on the way to a doctor's visit when her car ran off the road and into an embankment. The steering wheel crushed her chest, and she died instantly.

**"At only 23 years old, my mother left
five small children behind, and lots
of unanswered questions."**

All five children were in the car: James-5, Joel-4, me-3, John-2, and a newborn baby. Sidney, two months old, was adopted by my maternal grandparents.

As my mother was lying dead on the side of the road, two men in white held my arms as I was screaming, "I want my Daddy, I want my Daddy". I believe now that because I was at the innocent age of three, my cries reached the Throne of Father God in Heaven. We were all taken to the hospital. Joel had a broken leg; John had a head concussion. James and I escaped with only cuts and bruises; Sidney was found under the front seat.

> *Can a woman forget her nursing child, and not have compassion on the son of her womb? Surely, they may forget, yet I will not forget you.[16] See, I have inscribed you on the palms of My hands. Isaiah 49:15-16*

At the hospital, I was put in a room on a very tall bed. I remember it was very high off the ground, and my hip hurt every time I had to get down from the hospital bed to go to the bathroom. Soon, after we were released from the hospital, my father picked us up. I was told later in the years that there had been a custody battle. At the young age of 3. I was a little mother to my brothers. It was the beginning of feeling responsible and taking care of others.

Childen escape critical injuries

Mother of five killed in wreck near Stafford

Mrs. Martha Ann Laza, 22, of Houston died at 7:15 a. m. Wednesday morning about .2 mile west of Lester road in Stafford on Highway 90A when the car she was driving ran off the road and into an embankment.

With her were her five children, James McKay, 6; Joe Stephen McKay, 4; Rebecca Ann McKay, 2, and Sidney Laza Jr., about five weeks old. Joe Stephen received a broken leg and John David was admitted to the hospital for observation. He suffered a head injury. The other three children only received cuts and bruises.

Mrs. Laza apparently suffered chest injuries and died instantly. Justice of the Peace Roy Kelly of Stafford held the inquest at the scene.

Mrs. Laza is the wife of Stephen Joseph Laza, formerly of Needville. State Highway Patrolman Jerry Hancock who investigated said Laza told him that his wife had taken him to work earlier in the morning and apparently had gone home again. She was planning to go to the doctor in Richmond, he told the highway patrolman.

The victim is the daughter of Mr. and Mrs. J. C. Merchant of San Antonio.

Edward Wittneben of Needville dies

Funeral services for Edward Wittneben, 74, of Needville were held Thursday, August 12, at 2 p. m. from the Garmany and Co. Funeral Chapel in Needville. Mr. Don Martini officiated.

Mr. Wittneben passed away about 8:30 a. m. Tuesday. He was born near Welcome, came to Fort Bend County in 1919, and spent most of his life farming.

Survivors are a son, Edward Wittneben of Houston; two daughters, Mrs. Alice Meyen and Mrs. Lillie Meyen of Needville; three brothers, Willie Wittneben of Richmond, Henry Wittneben of New Ulm and Robert Wittneben of Welcome; two sisters, Mrs. Freida Kunkel of Olney and Mrs. Hattie Meier of Guthersville; nine grandchildren and two great-grandchildren.

Burial was in the Needville Public Cemetery.

Mrs. Martha Ann Laza of Houston died Wednesday morning when her [car ran off Highway 90A near St]afford about .2 mile west of Lester Road. Her five children escaped. One son received a broken leg and another son was admitted to the [hospital] with a head injury, but three other children received only minor cuts. [In the fore]ground are Sgt. Joe Mladenka of the Texas Department of Public [Safety and Justice of the] Peace Roy Kelly of Stafford who held the inquest. (Staff Photo)

NEWSPAPER ARTICLE
MOTHER OF FIVE KILLED IN CAR WRECK

CHAPTER 2

BEHIND THE MASK

In 1967, when I was five years old, we lived in Uvalde, where my father was a preacher at a small church. My five brothers and I all sat, lined up in the front row. Everyone always commented on Larry's obedient children. He wore us like a badge. We marched into the church single file. But what they didn't know was that in our house, it was church on Sunday morning, and the belt on Sunday afternoon. We were too young to know the circumstances in which we lived.

"We seemed like the perfect Christian family.
He swung his belt without mercy
and left whelps and bruises on us."

I vaguely remember a physical fight on our front porch between my father and my grandparents. I saw someone beating my

13

father with a rubber hose. It was my grandmother, but I didn't know her then. My brothers and I had been playing in the yard when we were rushed into the house. The front door hastily closed and locked behind us.

We heard a gunshot. Although I didn't know then, my grandmother fired a gun at my father, barely missing his head. After the fight and gunshot incident, we moved again. This time we moved to Houston, Texas, on Oxford Street. My father had a good job as a machinist, although he still preached on the weekends.

Our maternal grandparents, the Merchants, as we called them, once drove past our house, and James threw a rock at their car. We had been told that they were bad. My grandparents, my brother Sidney, and my mother's name were never spoken of again.

"It was as if my mother's existence

had become null and void,

and it felt like so had the biggest part of me."

My world was mostly my six brothers and me. We had each other, despite the challenges of living in a house with anger and abuse. Once, my father came home from work to find a small boot that had been drawn on the seat of one of the kitchen chairs. He immediately called each of us by name, one by one. We lined up in a row before him in full attention, military style. He asked each of us, starting with the oldest, down to the youngest, "Did you draw the boot on the chair?" Each of us answered, "No, sir." He promptly took off his belt.

Again, in a more threatening voice tone, he asked, which one of you drew a boot on the chair? No one answered. He said everyone would get a whipping until one of us told him the truth. So, he began with the oldest James, then Joel, John, Joseph, and Timothy. Then it was my turn. He asked me the same question: "Did you draw the boot on the chair?" I said, "No, sir." He proceeded to swing the belt across my legs and anywhere else it landed as I cried and screamed.

Finally, he stopped, grabbed James again, then Joel, and hit them. Seeing them hit and hurt, crying out for mercy and finding none. By the time he got to John, I couldn't stand it anymore. I yelled, "Stop, Dad, stop! I did it! I did it, just please stop hitting my brothers." He turned toward me and grabbed my arm, swinging the belt across my legs again. Now, he said, this is for lying. Even though I really didn't do it. I just hated seeing him hitting my brothers. I wanted to defend them somehow. My brothers didn't know why he treated me differently. Of course, I was the only girl, and my father told me I was special, and I believed him.

**"No one knew the price I had to pay
behind closed doors."**

Mark also escaped my father's aggressive fury because he was the youngest. He would spend hours with our father and was too young to know the pain my older brothers experienced, especially James, Joel, and John.

As far back as I can remember, every night, my father would come into my room. I was just a little girl. What could I do?

> *He who dwells in the secret place of the Most-High, shall abide under the shadow of the Almighty; 4He shall cover you with His feathers, and under His wings you shall take refuge;*
> *Psalms 91:1-4*

It was a secret pain and constant abuse. Although horrible things were happening to my body, it felt as if I would leave my body. I found out later that it is called detachment. But for me, it was the Holy Spirit carrying me into His Presence, where, in my mind and my heart, I was safe, and nothing could hurt me.

But I was still afraid to close my eyes. He was my father. A terrifying fear entered my heart. I was frozen with fear. I couldn't close my eyes to sleep because I never knew when my father would come into my room.

CHAPTER 3

FINDING HOPE IN DESPAIR

In August of 1968, while attending 1st grade at Field Elementary School, I met a friend, Brenda Andrews. She came from a troubled home, too. We got in trouble for arguing in class and were both sent to the principal's office. We had to hold the edge of our teacher's skirt all the way to the office. But by the time we left the office that day, we were best friends. Though we didn't see one another for many years after that season, we remained connected in the heart forever.

"It's amazing how two little girls, in the midst of trauma and domestic violence, found lifelong friendship."

We both lived in a dysfunctional home but were too young to know our lives were not normal. Brenda would load up a black trash bag full of toys and walk several blocks to my house so that we could play together. Sometimes, I was allowed to go to her house. I know she knew that something was not right in my house and that my father treated me differently, but we never talked about it. We fled to an imaginary world of fun and play.

My father was still a preacher, and we seemed to the world the perfect Christian family. He soon took a weekend pastor position at Pine Prairie Baptist Church in 1969.

"My six brothers and I sat quietly in the front row at every church service. No one knew the secrets behind the mask of seven well-behaved children."

We often disappointed the high standards set for preacher's kids. He paid the price for his unrealistic expectations for his children. I was told later that Deanna also suffered much horrific abuse at the hands of my father.

My father and stepmother fought behind closed doors. We would listen to them fighting through the walls of my bedroom. Their relationship worsened, and he turned to me. As early as I can remember, heartbreak and anguish filled my soul. He was my father. He told me not to tell. So, I carried the pain and secrets for such a long time.

The McKay family newspaper article announcing
Rev Larry McKay at Pine Parrie Baptist
Church in 1969

When I was about 8 years old, I was allowed to attend a Girls in Action (GA) Baptist summer camp.

It was as if God allowed me a temporary escape from the abuse and trauma in my home. I asked Jesus to live in my heart! I asked

> *"For God so loved the world, that He gave His only begotten Son, that whoever believes in Him shall not perish, but have eternal life* John 3:16 (NKJV)

him to please come and save me. His Presence of Hope, Great Mercy, and Love poured like oil upon my heart.

"As I sat by the campfire one night,
with a heavy heart and the Faith of a child,
I cried out to Jesus!"

The Church was my safe place, but at home, we lived in high alert. Sometimes, when my father was at work, our mom, Deanna, would let us go down the street to play baseball. I was always the last to be picked on the team. My brothers would say, Awe, we had her last time. But I loved being with my brothers. I was always the tag-along, big and little sister.

School was also our escape from our father. My 3rd-grade teacher, Mrs. Bailey, called me Smiley. She didn't know I was crying on the inside. No one knew. The anger and violent temper of my father would happen at any time. We never knew when or what to expect.

One day, Joel did something to anger my father when he grabbed my brother by the shoulders, banging his head against the glass window-framed kitchen door. My stepmother yelled for him to stop. I thought he was going to bust Joel's head open. Although most often, James and Joel got most of the physical abuse. Joel was especially verbally rebellious against my father's control.

My Nana (my father's mother) occasionally came to stay with us. She would always try to protect us from my father's rage and outbursts. I still had a big smile and a broken heart. No one knew. I just smiled on the outside, crying on the inside.

REBEKAH ON THE STAIRCASE LEADING UPSTAIRS
TO HER BROTHER'S ROOM.

24

One time, my Nana, James, and my other brothers were watching wrestling on TV together. Just as my father entered the house through the back door, he heard James say, "Damn." He immediately charged into the room and jumped on James, grabbing him by the throat. He began choking and shaking him. Our Nana pulled our father off him and made him stop.

My brothers often acted out in anger at school. The McKay kids had to leave school 5 minutes before the bell rang. I guess it was 5th grade. We all had to leave school early every day because my brothers would always get into fights after school. Now that I look back, I wonder why no one ever considered finding out Why did my brothers get into so many fights?

We lived in a two-bedroom house with the dining room converted into a third bedroom for me. My brothers slept upstairs in one large room with three sets of army bunk beds. I would hear my father's footsteps, climbing up the stairs in anger for something my brothers had done wrong. Or maybe because they were fighting among themselves. I would hear the screaming as he swung his belt at them to disperse his most used form of correction.

We didn't know why he was always so angry. It seemed everything was all our fault. I only knew that the more he turned to me, the less physical whipping I received, like my brothers. I would rather have had the belt than live in fear of his unwanted touches and control over my mind, emotions, and body.

"No one knew the price I had begun to pay
behind closed doors."

Once, Joel, in the 2nd grade, and John, in the 1st grade, ran away from home. They got miles away from the Houston airport. The police brought them back home. I have also wondered over the years why no one looked further into why two little boys would run away from home so young. They both got a beating, and my father shaved their heads as punishment. He made them stand in the front entranceway every day after school for weeks. They were both ashamed and wore hats to cover their heads at school so kids wouldn't laugh at them.

Even though life was hard, we found fun among ourselves when my father was at work. Being with my brothers was the only world I knew. There were some good memories amongst the bad. My father would take my brothers and me fishing at least once a month. We would go to the Texas City Dikes to fish off the rocks. My brothers loved to fish.

I fished too, but mostly, I tagged along to make sandwiches for my brothers. I even got good at baiting my fishing hook. But I eventually learned to hate Texas City Dikes, where my father would take me alone for more abuse. My brothers and I learned to survive together, apart from them. I was lost and afraid.

We went on family vacations; my brothers and I only had each other. Deanna, my stepmom, never came with us. Just my six brothers and me with our father. In addition, everyone played a musical instrument. My brother James played the clarinet; Joel, the trombone; and John played the trumpet and piano. John was the most gifted. He played the piano by ear and would play both the trumpet and piano at the same time. I tried to play the flute, but I wasn't as musically gifted as my brothers. I liked to draw. Art was my gift! My father would bring home a used instrument from the pawn shop, and whoever could play it would get to keep the instrument. My father played the saxophone and guitar. My brothers and my dad would sing in front of the church. No one knew what was behind the mask of this perfect musical Christian family. "I know God's hand was on me, protecting me from a hopeless destiny. "

God can't override another person's will. My father made horrible choices that harmed his children. But the good he gave me was life, music, and God! One day, I realized God had used my father to give me the gift of life, so I found my very breath and being in the presence of my creator, God. Secondly, during all the suffering and sorrow, I learned to sing to God through the tears. And he took us to God's house, where I learned about Jesus and met my real Heavenly Father, who would never abuse or abandon me.

CHAPTER 4

MY HERO BROTHER JOEL

By the end of the 1973 school year, Joel was 12, and I was 11; we graduated from 6th grade together at Berry Elementary. My brother Joel had failed second grade, so we were always in the same grade together. He was my protector and my best friend.

At school, he would always defend me, especially if a boy picked on me. One day, he decided to teach me how to defend myself. I only punched a boy one time. Since, no matter what, Joel was my defender!

**"With my brother Joel, I always felt safe.
He was tough and unafraid."**

But I never told him the terrible things Larry (our father) did to me. They were buried deep with shame, incomprehensible to process in the mind of a child. Unspeakable words, not to be spoken.

JOEL AND REBEKAH AT THEIR 6TH-GRADE GRADUATION TOGETHER

CHAPTER 5

SENT AWAY TO MEXICO

B y the end of the 1973 school year, Joel was 12. At the beginning of the summer, I was sent away to Monterey, Mexico, to spend the summer at my stepmother's aunt and uncle's home. No one asked me if I wanted to go. I didn't have a choice. Although my Aunt Pena didn't speak any English, my uncle did. It was an opportunity to learn a little Spanish. The first words I learned from my Tia Pena were sit down, be quiet, " and " move out of the way.

"Perhaps my stepmother knew what was happening to me, and maybe it was her way of trying to protect me."

Especially when she was cooking, she made homemade Mexican candy, which quickly became my favorite. It was a great experience of cultural diversity for my receptive mind. To get me out of the house, my Tia sent me with my uncle during the day. My uncle ran a restaurant in the downtown marketplace. So, I would go with him each day. I learned a few new words. It felt like an adventure.

It was like I was experiencing a brief escape from living in fear and control of my father! We went to a huge Catholic wedding, which I had never seen before. My Aunt took me to have my hair fixed, and I wore a pretty, pink dress.

After about a month, when my Tia was either gone or asleep, my uncle began to tell me to lie down on his bed. I obeyed. Abuse again, I was so confused. I couldn't understand. I guess I thought it was normal. I just pretended it didn't happen. I never told anyone. Whom could I tell? I felt nervous and uncomfortable. I just froze in fear. I just thought, I couldn't tell.

And yet somehow, as if to cover the heartbreaking secret torments in my young life. I was still smiling on the outside, crying on the inside.

Rebekah and her little cousin in Mexico

Chapter 6

Sent Away to Catholic School

Again, I was being sent away, this time to a Catholic Boarding School. We had often visited the nuns who had raised my stepmother. I still didn't understand why I was sent away. But I tried to see it as another kind of adventure, beyond my father's reach. The nuns made me a bedroom in one of the smaller classrooms. As the only student boarder, my heart felt sad and alone in the big hallways at night. I vividly remember going to the chapel down the long, dark hall early every morning and finding great comfort in my Heavenly Father. I would cry to Him and ask him to please help my daddy. I knew he was wrong, but I was powerless to change him or my circumstances.

I was afraid and would pray, begging God that my father wouldn't visit me. I felt ugly and sick inside whenever he came to see me. There was a small, fenced garden between the school and the convent. It was called Grotto. Inside the garden was a giant oak tree and a giant cross. Every morning and every night I would go to the garden. As I stood and gazed up at the cross, I felt His awesome presence. As a border, I was responsible for doing chores every day after school. I would mop the hallways and the winding steps. Stopping by the Chapel, always to peek in and tell Jesus, I loved him! It was there, in the garden, that I would spend hours talking to God, and His oil of comfort poured over my heart.

The Grotto was my safe place where God would be my comfort and strength. All the girls in 7th grade attended Charm class, we learned to walk down and up those stairs like a lady. I thought maybe someday my father would be proud of me.

After a few months, I don't remember why, but I returned home to the same life, and it was about to change again. I enrolled at Burbank Middle School with my brother Joel, my second school in the 7th grade.

Rebekah pictured with Deanna and the Nuns arriving at St Teresa Academy

CHAPTER 7

MY BURNING FATHER

My stepmother, Deanna, had begun working a full-time job, and my father's control over her and her income made their relationship worse. She threatened to file for a divorce. He countered her threat by pouring gasoline over his body and threatening to light a match.

> *God is our refuge and strength, a very present help in trouble. Psalms 46:1*
>
> *In that moment, God Himself was my Strength and my Ever-Present Help*

He lit the match while arguing and accidentally dropped it. In an instant, he was in flames. James, my oldest brother, grabbed a blanket to put out my burning father. As God would have it, at this moment, Joel, John, and I were at a weekend Baptist church camp. My earthly father had failed me, but my Heavenly Father was offering me something, something I would need to live, to survive, Himself through Jesus Christ. My faith grew, and I began a desperate dependency on God on the inside, while on the outside, it looked as if my life was hopeless.

It was not a coincidence that while my father was burning and being hospitalized, God was planting a seed of His love and Hope, deep within my soul. Upon my return home, I had no home anymore.

"My brothers and I were all sent to stay with church families, who willingly took us into their homes."

I didn't know where my brothers were staying. I was sent to stay with the Tasker family. They took me into their home and cared for me. I had to go to a new school again, my third school in 7th grade. And I longed for my brothers, my family. They had a daughter close to my age. Her name was Debbie. To me, she seemed to have everything: her own room, a canopy bed, and clothes, but most of all, she had a family. I reconnected with them years later to thank them for caring for me. They never knew the abuse we faced in our home, and I could never tell.

After a month or so, a person from the church came to get me one day to take me to visit my father in the hospital. I remember standing paralyzed by the door of his hospital room. I didn't want to go in. The person insisted, I entered the room slowly and stood at a distance from his bedside. My father motioned for me to come closer. I felt an overwhelming fear. I didn't want to go near him.

But he firmly motioned to me to come. I moved my feet, a step nearer to his bedside, close enough for him to grab hold of my hand. I tried to withdraw my hand from his peeling skin, but it was sickening. I cringed and gradually pulled back. He released my hand. We exchanged a few words; I don't remember what was said, just that I was relieved to get out of that room. It felt so full of despair and control. I felt sick inside.

**"Home as I knew it was no more.
I would never have my family together ever again."**

In the summer of 1975, after being released from the hospital, my father came to get me. He checked me out of school, even though it was almost summer break.

I was 13 now, and my life would change forever from this moment forward. I knew my life and his control over me were only beginning again. He said he wanted to keep all his kids together! We picked up my brothers, went to our old house, and were ordered to pack up everything we owned. We loaded everything into a moving truck all day. By that evening, we had driven to San Antonio, not knowing what was happening or why we were moving.

CHAPTER 8

ENTERING FOSTER CARE

We stopped by to visit my father's family and sold our washer and dryer, along with all our other household items. After a few days, my father put us all in the car and asked, "Which way do we go, Florida or California?" California, I blurted out. "California, it is", he said. My brother James had been staying with a family member in San Antonio. I guess my dad had deemed James defiant and left him in San Antonio. He was only 15 years old.

**"My stepmother came home from work
to find her house empty and her children gone. "**

We arrived in Los Angeles days later at 6:00 am on a Sunday morning. We stopped at a rest area, changed clothes, and went to church. We slept in the car that first night, my five brothers and I. After a week or two, my father had a job and leased a two-bedroom furnished apartment. My five brothers would share one of the bedrooms, and I would have the other. My father was supposed to sleep on the couch. But he didn't.

Our apartment was upstairs. One day, while walking up the stairs, my father slapped me on my bottom. There were kids around. I was embarrassed. The neighbor kids started talking about me. I felt dirty and ugly inside. I knew he didn't treat me like a daughter, more like a wife. I was glad when he left for work. I tried my best to cook for my brothers, but I was not very good at it. They would always ask my father, "Does Becka have to cook again?" My little brothers missed their mom. What could I tell them? Mark was only five. My father was gone working during the day. We were all alone.

**My older brothers and I began to question
my father's will, only to have our spirits
crushed by his overpowering control.**

Still, we went to church every Sunday to the Nazarene Church. Once, I was invited to go with the girls from church for a sleepover. My father said no because I was his little helper. I hated that he owned me. We talked among ourselves when he was gone, about a better life, trying to determine how we could escape the furious discipline of our father.

We moved again, this time to a big empty house with no furniture except for one couch and one bed in the front bedroom. My brothers all slept on the floor with just blankets. I was supposed to get the front room with the purple walls and the queen-size bed. My father was supposed to sleep on the couch, and again, he didn't. One morning, which was often, I awoke at 5 am with my father coming home and getting into bed.

I pretended to be asleep. He tried to pull me toward him. As he put his hands on me, I resisted and pulled away. I hated his control over me. I was afraid, but gathered up the courage to pull away. He responded, saying, "You're just like your mother; she was cold to me." Shocked at his words, I had seldom heard him mention her. But his hurtful, angry words made me know I had a mother and she had existed. In her defense, I blurted out, "Don't talk about my mother"! He kicked with his feet at full force, knocking me out of the bed.

For the first time, as I moved toward the bedroom doorway, I felt a growing inner strength to stand against him. It was now or never. He commanded me to stop. He said, "If you go out that door, never come back again." I reached for my packed suitcase, lying on the floor (previously packed), hoping to attend a youth church camp the following week. I had already defied my father; I couldn't back down now. I grabbed the handle of my suitcase, gathering a boldness from deep within, and I said," Well, then, I guess I won't come back". With those words, I ran to the back room where my brothers were sleeping. I awoke Joel and told him, "Come on, I'm leaving. I threw on a pair of pants under my nightgown. Joel and John both hurriedly got dressed. We ran past the front bedroom and out the front door. As we reached the front gate of the house, we heard my father yelling, "Get back in the house!"

We turned to see him standing in the doorway with a belt in his hand. It was dark outside, and we had nowhere to go. His voice of control won us over again. We retreated into the house. I guess he was too tired to hit us. I went back into the bedroom with a feeling of accomplishment. For the first time, I had refused his advances and control and lived. He slept on the couch that night.

The next day, he came home early and overheard us talking about wanting to live with our grandparents. I had given each of my brothers a dime to carry in their pocket and instructed them to use it only in case of emergency.

"My father grabbed Joel and began hitting him. I was afraid that, in his anger, he was going to kill my brother.

I asked John if he had his dime. He said yes, and I told him to run and call the police. I followed him. Soon, my father chased behind us. We had never run from him before. It felt like a bad dream, the wind pressing hard against me as I ran across a vacant field. Pushing John through a hole in the fence, even though afraid, we kept running.

We passed beyond return. We couldn't see our father behind us. John and I ran into a convenience store and hid behind the shelves. I told John to stay hidden and wait while I ran to the telephone booth to call the police. I told the lady on the phone that my father was beating my brother and was now chasing us. It seemed only minutes before the police came.

CHAPTER 9

TELLING THE SECRETS

On August 26, 1975, my brothers and I were taken into police custody immediately. I was now protected from my father, but lost all that was left of my family. For a little girl, it was a high price to pay for safety. They made me tell the secrets. I told them we were afraid of our father. Two investigators asked me questions for hours. I was tired, crying, and wanted to go home. I had to talk about all the years of the terrible things my father did. They kept asking me about every incident I could remember.

THE INTERROGATION OF A CHILD

Questioning me again and again. I didn't want to tell about the things my father did to my brothers and me. But they made me tell all of the secrets, about how he kept me home from school and took me down the old road by the church mission, when he would take me to where we used to go fishing at Texas City Dikes and park far away from people and how he would put his hands on me and touch me, how he rubbed himself against me.

It was a sick, dirty feeling. Exactly what did he do, they asked. Where did he touch you?

"They made me say the details.
They made me say the words. Reluctantly, I did."

It was hard to make words to describe what he did to me. I told them of the times he made me go to the grocery store with him. I didn't want to go. About how I always wore shorts or pants so maybe he wouldn't try to touch me. I sat so close to the passenger door to be out of his reach. So close, I thought I would fall out of the door. But he would give me orders to move over and sit next to him.

Reluctantly, I complied. We went to the store, bought groceries, and then he drove down the old dirt road of the Church Mission. It was late at night, and he would park and say he wanted to teach me things. He said I needed to know about things to become a lady one day. He said there is a difference between a woman and a lady. I was supposed to grow up and be a lady. I didn't understand most of what he talked about.

I wasn't present. He told me about his time in Japan during the war. The wives walk behind the husbands and serve them. He would always tell me that God had given me to him and that I belonged to him. He told me the Bible says I should obey my father. Now I know he used God's Word to manipulate and abuse me. He would say, "Come on, sis, sit next to daddy." I would be frozen in fear.

I remember one morning, I woke up and didn't have any clothes on. I couldn't understand why I was naked. I was confused. I don't think I ever slept soundly again. Always afraid to sleep. Sometimes, he would come into my room early in the morning and tell me You look just like your mother. I slept with my hair up on my pillow, and he would say, Your mother used to do her hair like that. A few years before he took us to California, my brothers and I were looking through a dresser and found a picture of our mom and dad.

I longed to know her, but I only knew Deanna as my mother. And I couldn't tell her. I thought she loved my little brothers, but not me. He never let us be close. He kept me with him most of the time, except while he was at work. I found out years later, when I wondered why Deanna didn't protect me, that she had faced her own abuse from my father. Saying the words of what he did was hard; I didn't want to admit it happened to me. I felt ugly and dirty. Writing these words in this book at the beginning was challenging for me, but it is crucial to bring dark things into the light. It was as if we began living life in a kaleidoscope of changing environments, people, and places, with no stability and no solid ground beneath our feet. Separated by distance, I lost my only family left: my brothers. Under the Shadow of the Almighty was where I would learn to find great comfort inside myself for years.

**"Now I know it was as if I were in a bubble,
and all these terrible things happened to someone else.
I would leave my body and be carried away
in my mind into the Secret Place,"**

I don't remember exactly when the abuse began. Maybe six, seven, or eight years old. I think it was gradually worse. I now know there was a lot of grooming and manipulation. It happened the earliest I can remember. He told me not to tell. That I was the only one he could turn to. He said, "I need you to help daddy". It was gross and sick. I would leave my body, fondled and abused, to a safe place in my heart where nothing could hurt me, with Jesus. I told them that he would come into my room after getting off work early in the morning, after dropping my stepmother off at work.

I talked about the times when my stepmom was at work, and all my brothers were at school, year after year, day after day. He would make me stay home from school. My brothers would say," Why does Becka get to stay home from school?" Oh, how I longed to go to school!

They didn't know. And I was powerless to change anything. After everyone left for school, he would bring me into his and Deanna's bedroom. He would sit on the bed and pull me in front of him, opening his pants, and rub against me…so gross.

He would then cry hysterically and say he was sorry. He kept saying he needed me. I was the only one he could turn to. He said, "You are not wrong; I am." You are just helping daddy. He would tell me this was our secret. I never wanted to tell anyone, not even myself. He continued to quote scripture to me to justify his actions. Even sleep and rest are taken for granted by most people, but not me. I would live in anticipation of the worst. It's only God's Grace that I developed the coping skill of finding the good in every terrible situation. Sometimes they were much more complex than others, and I would lie myself on the Mercy Seat of God (Not really knowing what that meant). I would put my head in God's lap. I thought God's throne looked like Abraham Lincoln's gigantic statue, but I knew deep down that God's throne is real.

For you have been my hope, Sovereign LORD, my confidence since my youth

Psalms 71:5

"I believed God followed me everywhere, just like the moon, wherever I would go."

He would tell me to wash and then take me to a store to buy something. He wanted me to walk close to him in the mall. I walked a few steps away from him. He would get mad and pull me to put his arm around me as we walked. I hated it, but what could I do? I was only a kid, and no one would listen to me. It is essential to know that one of the most hopeless feelings as a child is when you are crying out in every way you know, and it feels like no one is listening. As I write these words, sharing my story, perhaps someone is listening to me now! Now it seemed as if everything was all, my fault. I was separated from all I knew and loved...my brothers. I didn't know where they took them. The detectives took me in a van to MacLaren Hall Detention Center in Orange County, California. I was told there was no home for me. On the way, they talked and laughed, as I sat alone in the back seat, crying.

Two ladies instructed me to take off my clothes. They strip-searched my body. I felt embarrassed taking off all my clothes in front of two strange women whom I didn't know. They took my clothes and gave me someone else's clothes to wear. I was just a little girl, devastated. What did I do wrong?

Why was I being punished? And where were my brothers? I was there for three days until they found a foster home for me. When I got to the foster home, I had nothing. No brothers, no mother, no father, no belongings from my house, and not even my own clothes.

> *And everyone who has left houses or brothers or sisters or father or mother or wife or children or fields for my sake will receive a hundred times as much and will inherit eternal life.*
>
> *Matthew 12:29*

CHAPTER 10

A BRIEF TASTE OF FREEDOM

When you come into foster care in California, they give you a $50 clothing voucher. So, the foster mom took me to buy a few things to wear. There were about 3 or 4 other teenage girls in this foster home. For the first time in my life, I heard secular music and listened to popular teen, non-Christian music on the radio. It was like, for a moment, I was free for the first time in my life. The girls took me to the beach. I got to get a bathing suit. I had never had one before. It was summertime, and I got some shorts too. I had never been able to wear cool clothes.

But after a couple of weeks of experiencing freedom, the reality came back to me. I missed my brothers, and I still wanted to go home, not to my father, but to my only family, my brothers. Losing my parents was okay for me, but losing my brothers was like losing myself. The most significant part of my identity was being the only girl among all my brothers. We always took care of one another. And at least, even in dire situations, we were together. I was a mom to my brothers.

Without them, I would be so lost. I was just a little girl, devastated. What did I do wrong? Why was I being punished?

It seemed like we would go to court in only a few days or a few weeks. They wanted me to testify against my father, but I refused. Somehow, I still felt obligated to protect him. I felt responsible. In the court hallway, I saw him. I was still afraid of him, but although I hated what my father did to me, I still loved him very much. Someone gave me a note from my father. The note said, "I want to be buried next to your mother". I'm not sure why they allowed him to send me the note. But it made me very sad. The judge declared my father unfit; now we were wards of the state of California. A temporary conservatorship was granted to Texas, and we were sent to San Antonio to live with our maternal grandparents. My stepmother was given custody of my three younger brothers, Joseph, Timothy, and Mark. She was their mother, and they were her sons. For some reason, she wasn't our mother anymore.

My grandparents didn't know us, and we didn't know them. And they didn't know how to handle four damaged teenagers, ages 12, 13, 14, and 15. We arrived by plane and were excited about a new life without our father's rage and control.

We were happy to see each other and our big brother James. James had been living on his own but came to live with my grandparents. It was a bit awkward being with our new brother, Sidney. He was excited to have brothers and a sister for the first time. But the reunion was more complicated for all of us than we had imagined. We didn't know him, and he was young and didn't know the life we came from or have any of our shared sibling experiences. We were enrolled in school. My brothers went to Terrell Wells Middle School, and I was enrolled back at St Teresa's Academy again.

The first weeks were full of catching up on stories about the mother we had never known. My Grandfather told me that at my mother's funeral, I was crying and screaming I want my mommy. He had the coffin opened so I could see my mom one more time.

We were told lots of terrible stories about our father. Our grandmother showed us pictures of our mom and us. It was a strange feeling, like meeting someone for the first time, but that already died many years ago. My grandparents went to the Adams family cemetery, where my mom is buried. We attended the Annual Tomlinson Cemetery Association meeting.

I saw my mother's grave for the very first time. Feeling a connection to my mother and seeing her grave was all surreal. It was there that we met other family relatives. Many of them recognized me and said, I looked just like my mother. I was happy inside that I looked like my mother. It felt like I belonged, and she was with me, part of me. They told me more stories about my mom. I hung on to every word. How can you desperately miss someone you have never known? I just missed her! "My grandmother would sometimes take us to Ravenhill Baptist Church. No matter how hard life was, it was like being home to be in my Father God's house."

They had an altar call, and I went forward. I wanted to make sure that God knew I belonged to Him! Jesus was saving me again, in the midst of great pain and sorrow.

CHAPTER 11

BROKEN PLACEMENTS

But after a short time at our grandparents', with all the stories and family history lessons, we began to learn quickly why our mom had run away from that house to get married at the age of 16. We would spend at least once a month at the cemetery, cleaning around the headstones and weeding. My grandmother was angry and bitter.

She would get angry at our behaviors and say ugly things, like "You are just like your father, McKay trash. I wouldn't spit on him if he were on fire." I don't know if she knew he had really been on fire before. She and my grandfather had planned to adopt us. She hated the McKay name. She would say, you can't help where you come from, but you can rise above it". We were constantly taunted about our father and Deanna, too! She said mean things about my little brothers, Joseph, Timothy, and Mark. She hated our father; I thought she hated me. She told us stories about our mom and dad. She said my dad ran my mom off the road, and because of him, she died.

In November of 1975, my Nana and Papa (my paternal grandparents) were on their way home from my aunt's house. An oncoming vehicle had its bright lights on, causing it to run off the road into a ditch. They were both killed. Our maternal grandparents, The Merchants, didn't want to let us go to the funeral. But eventually, they let us go only to the funeral service.

They wanted us to sign the guest book with the last name Merchant. I thought it would be hurtful to my Nana and Papa's family. But I think I did. James refused and signed his name, James McKay. Soon afterwards, I found all my school papers with my last name, McKay, marked out with a black marker. Our stay with our grandparents was short-lived, as was to become the pattern for us; no place was to be home for long.

I found comfort in the Chapel and Grotto
at St Teresa's Academy School.
It was a place of refuge.

Now it was a refuge from my grandmother's anger and bitterness. I was a cheerleader. My grandmother made me cheerleading bloomers to wear under my uniform skirts. At first, it was a great idea, until the day I came home and all my panties were cut up in my drawers. I asked her what happened, and she told me I could wear my cheerleading bloomers for panties.

I said I can't because they are too big to wear under my pants. I cried and cried. See, I told her my pants look all puffy with cheerleading bloomers as panties. How could you tear up my panties? Such was the crazy life I was living. It was a nightmare that just kept getting worse. She finally bought me some big granny panties to wear.

But the Lord has been my defense, And my God the rock of my refuge.
Psalm 94:22

One day, I went to get my little white Bible; it was the only thing my dad had given me. It was gone. I asked her where it was, and she said she'd thrown it away because nothing from that McKay trash was allowed in her house. I guess that meant me too. If he was trash, then that meant so was I.

I loved my time at St Teresa Academy and wearing my school uniform. It gave me a sense of belonging. It is where I once found great comfort. We had a candy fundraiser for my school, and I won 1st place for selling the most candy! I would go to the flea market on the weekends with my grandfather and sell the candy. I won $25 and bought myself a dress and some shoes! But my joy was not to last; my grandmother was very prejudiced.

One day in January of 1976, my grandmother picked me up from school and saw me talking to my friends (who happened to be Hispanic), and she got mad at me. She was extremely prejudiced. The next day, she checked me out of St Teresa's Academy school and sent me to Terrell Wells Middle School. At least, I would get to be with my brother Joel. This was my second school, in 8th grade, I followed Joel everywhere. He hated it. He would always say, "Stop following me," but I followed right behind him anyway. For a short time, it was like it had always been, since 2nd grade, we were together.

Joel was my special brother, and he had become the only constant in my life. Meanwhile, our time at our grandparents' house got worse. Joel and I often conflicted with my grandmother's bitterness and anger. She would lock us outside the house in the hot sun all day. If we questioned her authority, she would get a switch off the tree and hit us with it! Joel would just run away. Finally, he left, and I didn't see him anymore.

My mom's brother, my Uncle Neal, and his wife, Betty, asked if I could stay with them. So, my grandmother said yes. I was so relieved and happy. My Aunt Betty and Uncle Neal were very friendly to me. I thought I was going to get to have a life now. But as always, my time at my aunt's house was short. We spent my first day at my aunt's house, trying on a pair of my cousin's jeans and putting on makeup.

That day, we had to go to my grandmother's house. I begged my aunt, please, not to take me over there. But she did. My grandmother saw the makeup on my face and sent me to the bathroom to scrub it off. She said I couldn't go with my Aunt Betty anymore. I was afraid of my grandmother. She called herself old, mean grandma. She even signed our birthday cards as old mean grandma.

My grandmother made me roll my hair every night like she did when I was 3 years old. I saw pictures of me with Shirley Temple curls. But I was a teenager now, and ringlet curls were not in style. One night, it was late when I took a bath and washed my hair. I asked my grandmother, "Can I please go to school one day with normal hair?" My hair is still wet, and it won't dry by morning if I roll it now. She said no, I had to roll my hair. I refused, saying, "I can't; my hair is still wet." Even as I pleaded with her, she didn't understand. I was in the 8th grade and just wanted to be normal! But as I pleaded, my hair, of course, was drying, so I would go into the bathroom and wet my hair again.

My grandmother insisted that I roll my hair. Finally, she called my grandfather to come and roll my hair. I said Grandpa, I want to go to school with normal hair. Why do I always have to roll my hair? He said we are not going to adopt you and give you the name Merchant. I yelled, "I don't want your name. My name is McKay. With that last remark, my grandpa swung his fist at me and hit me in the nose. Blood went everywhere, all over my nightgown. My little brother John ran into the living room to defend me. Stop hitting my sister, he said. I ran to the telephone to call the police. My grandmother got the other phone and hung up. Finally, I managed to get the police, and they arrived at our house shortly after.

"I came to the door with blood still all over my nightgown
and told the police what happened.
They just looked at me and said,
"This is a family matter," and left me there."

The next day, instead of going to school, I ran away to my dad's sister's house, my Aunt Gay Lynn's. I called the CPS social worker and told her I am no longer staying at my grandparents' house. In January 1976, a top chart song by Diana Ross was "Do You Know Where You're Going To?" I would sing the words and cry to God! I only had his Hope and nothing else about where I was going to lay my head to sleep and wake the next day. The song's words echoed in my mind, asking the questions to which only God had the answers!

Do you know where you're going?
Do you like what life is showing you?
Where are you going to, do you know?

Do you get what you're hoping for?
When you look behind you, there's no open door.
What are you hoping for, do you know?

Child Protective Services finally came to get me and placed me at my dad's other sister's house, my Aunt Arlene's. I was enrolled at Southside Middle School. But my stay at my aunt's didn't last too long. I remember being very sad and spending time lying on my bed, just listening to music. I was depressed and cried a lot. The welcome mat did not last beyond a couple of months. They had two boys and an adorable one-year-old girl. They had their family, and I didn't fit in. It was almost summertime, and I was sent to an emergency foster home.

We were placed in separate homes, with various relatives and institutions. No one wanted three teenage kids, one temporary placement after another with different relatives. The welcome mat and sympathy for a troubled teenager were always short-lived.

**"At fourteen years old, again, there was no place for me.
I didn't understand why no one wanted me."**

I only knew I could cry to Jesus. I cried out to God during those years for help! Still, I remember feeling as if my pain was not to be in vain, that in the midst of sorrow, my Heavenly Father had a special plan for me. I cried to Him each night, for so many years, and found great comfort in clinging to hope for tomorrow. The tomorrow I knew God would give me if I could hold on to His promise of faith, hope, and love.

As the state ran out of placements for me, I was taken to the Romero family's home, which was an emergency shelter and foster home. It was nice, but one more stranger's house on my journey. There were other children like me, only much younger.

"It was here, in the Romero foster home

that I found my call and great comfort in sharing the love

and compassion of Jesus with the little ones

who had no fathers or mothers."

I thought to myself, how sad it was that they didn't have their mothers and fathers. I didn't know about the fact that I didn't have a mother or father anymore either.

Nurturing and loving them gave me purpose during my own hopeless situation, but I always missed my brothers and longed to belong to a family again. I asked my case worker, Ms. Davis, if I could see my brothers. She told me that it

God of all comfort, who comforts us in all our tribulation, that we may be able to comfort those who are in any trouble, with the comfort with which we ourselves are comforted by God.
2 Corinthians 1:4

was too much paperwork. And so, I didn't see my brothers for months, and then it turned into years.

CHAPTER 12

BUCKNER BAPTIST GIRLS HOME

My journey through foster care was, at its heart, a home search, a place to belong, and to become myself. Still, my world was ever-changing. It was like living in a different world, with no brothers, no home, or family. I thought about my brothers all the time. It felt like they were on the other side of the world. My heart was beyond broken without them. I was so confused. I cried myself to sleep at night and wondered, How can you get a new family? I felt lost in a world of new places and strangers. Even though I really tried hard to fit into this family. But, inside, it was only an emergency shelter foster home. Until they, the state, could find a placement for me. If only I could find adequate words to communicate the magnitude and lifelong devastating effects of separating siblings.

Consistent sibling visits were not practical after my brothers were sent back to California. Our sibling relationship was forever changed. We lost the close bond we had as children. We each went on to live separate lives. For many years in early adulthood, we only saw one another at Christmas and my maternal grandmother's. But after her passing, we never stayed connected. We rarely see one another as adults. I lost my family forever.

"I remember thinking it wasn't fair,

that everyone else gets to have a family and a home,

but I had to have a placement."

Once again, my stay was short. I had lost count of the number of placements, as they called them. In a child's thinking, to me, a place mat was the thing that goes on the dining room table.

At 14, going from placement to placement, I was sent to live at Buckner Baptist Children's Home. I left some of my stuff at every placement. I used to think I was like Hansel and Gretel, leaving breadcrumbs to find my way home. Maybe that's why I forgot a little of my stuff at every home. Maybe one day, I could follow the trail of my belongings to find my way home. I felt like a deck of cards, shuffled from place to place. Not belonging anywhere. Feeling alone in the world without a home.

I became numb. Processing losing my family and home. I knew my family situation was bad. But nothing could compare to nothingness. I was shown my room, with beds neatly lined up against the wall. I thought to myself, real homes don't have this many beds.

But there was one good thing. I would get to see my brother, Joel, on Sundays at church. He was placed at Buckner Baptist Boys Home.

"We would be bused to Trinity Baptist Church
on Sundays so that I would see Joel!"

I looked forward to every Sunday; it was not only my favorite day to be at God's house, but also the day when Joel and I could sit together during the church service.

I started the 9th grade at Robert E. Lee High School. All the kids knew we came from THE HOME. The massive pillars on either side of the entrance gate reminded you that you were NOT at HOME, but entering THE HOME. We were ashamed and embarrassed.

It is a simple word, THE, but it mattered so much to me. I thought, if I could take THE from in front of the word HOME, then I could be at HOME again. It's funny how you feel as a kid. I want people to hear these words and better understand the child's view!

The girl's home was an eye-opening experience for a young girl who had lived such a sheltered life under my father's control. The girls at the Girls' HOME cursed and talked back to adults, and smoked cigarettes. My brothers and I didn't dare talk back to an adult. I certainly didn't curse, and I had never listened to any music except for Hymns from church. But to fit in, I learned quickly how to open a pack of cigarettes and try smoking pot in the closet with the other girls in the home.

"As God is with us during every challenge,
He was with me then.
He sent someone to show His love for me."

I didn't seem to fit there either. I wanted to be different. And I knew I was different. My friend Barbie and the girls all tried to express themselves and be heard! Our approach was not the most appropriate, nor was that of the other girls, who would sneak out at night through the bedroom window.

The home was filled with troubled girls, each struggling with challenging behaviors that reflected their deep pain and longing for family. Their actions, often misunderstood or deemed inappropriate, were desperate cries for family connection and belonging.

Joel and I were the only two siblings still kind of together. We were rarely allowed to visit our little brother John. He was placed in a group home in Kerrville. One Sunday, excited to see Joel, I went to sit in our usual seats, and he was not there. He had been sent back to California. My brother Joel was all I had left of my family, and now he was gone. As I sat through the service that day, tears streamed down my face as my heart was breaking, My heart wanted to burst! Now, I had lost everything and everyone. He was the last member of my family. How would I grow up without him? I felt abandoned and without hope, powerless to fix my family. Even, the horrific abuse was not as hard as this.

I remember going up to the front of the church with my brother Joel in response to an altar call. I would hear in my heart, God calling my name. Rebekah, I will never leave you, nor forsake you! God reminded me that I was his child, and I believed in Jesus.

There is a friend who sticks closer than a brother.
Proverbs 18:24

In that Moment, God Himself was closer than a brother.

CHAPTER 13

THE ART EASEL GIFT

Art was my gift from God and my therapy. I remember thinking that real artists had an art easel. If I had an art easel, then I could be a real artist like my mother. There was an art studio at the girl's home. I used to love going there to draw and paint.

The Browns were the house parents at a maternity home for girls on the same property. They were also overseers of the Art studio room. They used to let me come anytime I wanted to draw or do craft projects.

Mr. Brown knew I loved art! On my 15th birthday, he told me that he had something for me in the garage. I followed him to find a beautiful gift of a wooden stick easel. To someone else, it probably wasn't much. But to me, it was a special gift of confidence and hope for my artistic destiny!

I don't know if Mr. Brown knows the Gift he gave me that day, but his act of kindness forever touched my life. When I ran away from the girl's home, I carried that wooden art easel with me on the Greyhound bus back to Houston. His gift of inspiration was that one day, I could grow up to be a graphic artist! Many years later, I did!

"It was in that simple gift

of a wooden art easel, that I discovered

the gift of creative expression."

This small, inexpensive token of kindness would be a gift I would carry with me for the rest of my life. Art became a way of life for me. It was a therapeutic tool God used to bring healing to my mind and soul.

THE WOODEN ART EASEL

CHAPTER 14

BLESSINGS IN THE STORM
GOD'S PROMISE

Even with a place to draw and express my sorrow creatively, nothing could replace the loss of family, and especially my brothers. January 12, 1977, on my 15th birthday at Buckner Baptist Children's Home. Overwhelmed with grief and loss, I walked the fence line of that children's home late one night, screaming, crying out to God, "God, I know you saved me when I was eight, but could you come save me again. Father God, please come and save me again. I promise to come back and help the others. And I will tell them it was you!

**"I cried out, Please God, don't leave me here
in a children's home. I never forgot the
promise. I made to God that night."**

And His promise to me, that if I would trust Him, He would rescue me. He would use my life to help many others. And I have never forgotten from where He brought me. And by His Grace, I have come back to help others.

I remembered that it had been during a church service that my brother Joel and I were drawn to the altar, in need of HOPE and God's

> *...being born again, not of corruptible seed, but of incorruptible, by the Word of God which lives and abided forever.*
> *1 Peter 1:23*
>
> *In that moment, God's Word became life and breath to my very soul.*

Love. Rev. Buckner Fanning of Trinity Baptist Church welcomed us warmly and handed each of us a copy of The Living Bible. Inside the front cover of my Bible, he had written...

**"God will use this book
to bless you all the days of your life."
Buckner Fanning**

Those words became a promise that carried me through the chaos and uncertainty of my world. As I read, the scriptures came alive, offering hope and comfort when I needed it most.

Nearly 30 years later, I came back to tell him Thank you for giving me that Living Bible. I tried to contact him and left a message at his office. I wanted to tell him that the words did indeed come off the page and had become life and breath to me. I stopped at a coffee shop, and as I entered through the door, there was Rev. Buckner, standing right in front of me! I told him I had been trying to make an appointment to see him. He was so kind and humbly receptive to listening to my words. We got our coffee and sat down on the patio.

God had made my appointment for me. I shared with Rev. Buckner that 30 years before, I had been at the Buckner Baptist Girls' Home and had been bused to his church on Sundays. We sat and talked for about 30 minutes. I will never forget his warm welcome and his kindness in taking the time to hear my heart and speak words of wisdom into my life. I would see him again several times throughout the following years. But to one child, his fatherly love and kindness were just like that of Jesus!

During my time of transition from living in a broken family to living in a broken system, I ran to the only one I knew was with me all along. I was on my own now, and only God would protect me from the life I could have accepted as my life's reality.

His gifts of perseverance, faith, hope, and LOVE sustained me on the inside, even as my world looked hopeless from the outside.

A few months later, my 9th-grade school year was almost over. I couldn't stay at the girl's home anymore. I didn't want to become something I wasn't, to find solutions to life problems in inappropriate ways, like many of the girls at the home. I ran away again, to try to find a place to belong.

Chapter 15

A Picture of a Family

Finally, the Romeros, my foster family, granted me permission to return and live at their house. The state had told them that if they were no longer an emergency foster care home, then I could stay. For me, their home was a kind of normalcy, a structured family life where there was love and kindness.

I remember seeing my foster dad hug my foster mom in the kitchen while she was cooking. I didn't really understand what I was seeing. Only thinking "when I grow up someday, I want to have that. When I grow up, I'm going to be a foster parent." Now I know what I saw that day.

"In that moment, there was a window of hope.

I saw a picture of a family.

A picture of what maybe I could have someday."

Maybe they both know now, the incomprehensible gift, unseen to the naked eye. But this child was forever touched.

It was the beginning of summer, and I got a summer youth job, earned money, and bought my own school clothes. I started 10th grade at Edison High School. A new school again. But this time, I wanted to try to fit in better. I joined the pep squad, and my foster mom helped me learn to sew. A lifelong skill, I still treasure today. I made my own uniform and sewed most of my summer clothes. They had big family gatherings at Canyon Lake. There were lots of relatives and kids running around. It was the first time I saw a family having fun together.

But by the end of the year, MaryAnn, my foster mom, was going to have another baby. It was a boy. A lot of relatives came to congratulate her and my foster dad. I overheard one relative say, "Well, I guess you have your pair now!" They already had two girls and a boy, so this baby boy made it a pair of each. Which, in my young trauma mind, they really meant, Rebekah, you don't really belong. You are not included in the sibling count of this family.

Christmas with the Romero Family

I felt like I had pretended they were my real family long enough, and I didn't really belong. Now I am 16 years old, and it was close to the end of my 10th-grade year. I had survived loneliness, despair, abandonment, and sexual abuse, but a deep underlying sadness filled my heart. I grieved the loss of my brothers, my family as I had known it to be. Even though there was abuse in our home, I would have endured it if only I could have kept my brothers together. I never had time to grieve the loss of my family. I was busy struggling to survive.

Final report cards will be coming soon. I didn't think I did so well in my grades, and I had begun skipping classes. One day, I took my foster dad's liquor in a can to school and drank it with orange juice to numb the pain. I spent most of the day on the floor in the girls' bathroom, sick and wanting to die. I just wanted to go to Heaven, where I could see Jesus and not have to cry anymore.

I felt like a disappointment to the Romero family, my brothers, my God, and myself. So, I awoke early one morning before anyone else, packed a few clothing and items I could carry on a bus, including my art easel, and ran away. Never to return to the Romero foster family again. I wanted to go back to Houston, to be with my own family, to find what was left of it.

I went to stay with a friend from school. Ana Gonzalez. Her family took me in, and we would go to Piedras Negras, Mexico, on the weekends. They owned a donut shop, and I spent some days that summer helping my friend Ana at work. I was in deep depression, not knowing where I was supposed to go. Where would I live? Where did I belong?

I took a bunch of Aspirin and other pills I could find, and I wanted to die. But I didn't, just horribly sick and throwing up. One spot of joy was that I loved helping take care of a friend's two-year-old nephew. Tragically, after I left Ana's house to go back to Houston to find my family, the little boy was killed by an exploding water heater. Someone called me to come to the funeral, but I just couldn't.

**"Every night, I placed my face on my pillow
to muffle the sounds of my heart's cries to God."**

All through the years, every day, I felt empty inside, a longing to belong. For years, in the girl's home, every foster home, every relative placement, everywhere I went, every night, I cried myself to sleep.

Hoping I could wake up and be home again. Like Dorothy of The Wizard of OZ, it was all just a bad dream. She woke up, and she was home again. I longed to be home.

Debbie, a girl from the Girls Home, had gone to live with her grandmother in the country, just outside of San Antonio. I called her, and her grandmother said I could stay with them for a little while. So, I went to stay with her and found a summer babysitting job. My friend, Debbie's grandmother, took me to the interview, and I got the job. Every Sunday night, her grandmother would take me to the babysitting job, and I would stay and work for the week. Her grandmother would pick me up on Friday nights. I earned $50 per week.

By the end of the summer, I had saved enough money to buy some clothes and a one-way bus ticket back to Houston.

CHAPTER 16

LOOKING FOR A PLACE CALLED HOME

I wanted to go home to Houston and see my little brothers, Joseph, Timbo, and Marky. I didn't know then that I couldn't save my brothers; only God could do that. I called my stepmother, Deanna, to tell her I would be moving to Houston.

When I arrived at the bus stop in Houston, I took another bus to St. Joseph's Hospital, where my stepmother worked. I told her I came to help her with my brothers. But although I tried, I couldn't even help myself, much less help rescue my little brothers. I was running from the pain of heartbrokenness.

Once, Deanna tried to send me to see a counselor. I told the counselor that I would talk about anything except for my father. I still felt a need to protect him and the horrible truth of what had happened to our family, to me! As soon as she mentioned my father, I ran out of the counseling room. I know that I had the best counselor, His name was Jesus!

It was 1978, and I enrolled at Spring Branch Senior High School as a junior. I had just turned 17 and was trying to start a new life. My little brothers were not doing too well. Joseph, 15, was hospitalized for his safety and was in and out of recovery programs for youth. Timothy was 14, and Mark was just 11.

Somehow, my father found out where my stepmother lived. He had come to see my younger brothers while I was away. My brothers told me later that my father wanted to see me. He wanted his family back together. The phone rang, and I answered. It was him. He said he was going to come see me tomorrow. I was still afraid of him and didn't know how to respond. I just uttered the word Okay and hung up the phone. Early the next day, no one was at my stepmother's apartment except me.

I heard him knocking at the door, calling my name. Rebekah Ann, he called my name again. The door was locked. My heart was beating out of my chest. I ran to hide in my stepmother's closet and prayed to God that he would go away. I didn't want to see him. I sat there for hours until my stepmother came home from work. I told her that he had come and that I was afraid of him. I didn't hear from him again until years later.

My stepmother worked a full-time job and did her best to care for three boys on her own. She sincerely wanted to protect Mark from the same outcomes as Joseph and Timothy, so she placed him at Boys' Country, a Christian children's home for boys.

I felt sad that I couldn't help my brothers. I found a friend in school, Rosie Gonzalez. She had a 2-year-old son with her stepfather. Her mom had died several years before. We immediately bonded through our mutual trauma.

In all your ways acknowledge Him, And He shall direct your paths.
Proverbs 3:6

"We would cruise the streets at night searching for something or someone, trying to find a place to belong."

After a few months of late-night parties and finding only more emptiness, I knew I didn't belong with this group of kids, and the direction we were going was nowhere. Something inside made me think I had to decide on my future. And I knew God had a destiny for me. And although I loved my friend Rosie.

I knew she didn't want to go or understand that God had something better for us. And so, I made a hard decision not to answer the phone the next time Rosie called me late at night to go cruising the streets.

When I wrote the poem, I thought it was for Rosie, but now I believe it was really written for both of us.

I am but an angry child,
roaming hopelessly, running wild.

I am but a starfish, lying on the beach,
no nurturing waters within my reach.

I am but a sunflower seed enchanted,
No chance to grow, never to be planted.

REBECKA, AGED 16

Rosie, age 17, and Rebekah, age 16

God was telling me that I couldn't help anyone unless I let him teach me how to help myself. My favorite class was art. My teacher knew the trauma that I had come from my background. She would let me go for walks to draw whenever I just needed time alone with God. God was always so merciful to me, placing someone on my path to show me grace and compassion. I learned early to recognize the angels in disguise, sent to me as comforters by Father God.

Still, I was very independent, and I got a job on the weekends at a sandwich shop about eight blocks from my stepmother's apartment. The sandwich shop was open until 1 am on Friday and Saturday nights. I would have to clean up after closing, so it was at least 2 am by the time I finished. My positive influence friends from school, Bobby and Leonard, would always stop by the sandwich shop for a soda on weekends. Bobby would always give me a ride home. Sometimes, he would take Leonard home, then come back to pick me up. We sat in his car and talked about life, our dreams, and our hopes.

One day, I was sharing my dream of becoming an artist and an ad man, and Bobby mentioned his mom works in advertising. He would ask his mom to help me. And she did! I got an interview for a job at the newspaper next to Spring Branch High School, doing advertising. I showed up with no experience but a lot of enthusiasm. I told Mr. Finch, the Advertising Manager, "I don't know anything about advertising, but I am willing to work hard and learn." The manager said He would give me two weeks to see what I could do. An open door was all I needed. I learned to operate the production camera and create graphic artwork for newspaper ads. Every day was like going to advertising class! This was my first of many jobs in advertising and marketing.

"My friend Bobby's presence in my life felt like a Godsend, bringing a bright spot amid my despair and loss."

Once, when he and Leonard brought me home from work, we sat for a while, all talking in the driveway. Then he said, "You want to go with me to take Leonard home?" I said, "Yes, " which was funny because he had just brought me home. After we dropped Leonard off at his house, we headed back to mine. We laughed and talked and talked, or probably I did most of the talking! But sometimes, we didn't talk at all. We just quietly sat together. When we got back to my stepmom's house, he parked in the driveway. We both got out of the car and sat outside for a while. When he was about to leave, I reached out to hug him. He was tall and handsome. He looked down at me and gave me a gentle, sweet, simple kiss. Then he looked at me and said, "We have something special here!" I said, "Yes, we do!" Then he said, if we were to be boyfriend and girlfriend and then we broke up, we wouldn't like each other anymore. So, we can't ruin something so special. I will never forget that moment.

We promised each other we'd stay forever friends, clinging to the comfort of that bond as everything else around us felt uncertain. But as the school year wore on, reality settled in, and I couldn't fix my family, no matter how much I wished I could. Deanna tried to guide me, offering instructions and advice, but I had been navigating life on my own for so long that her attempts felt foreign and overwhelming. I pushed back, resisting her control over my comings and goings, desperate to hold onto the little independence I had carved out for myself.

CHAPTER 17

WHAT IS A MOTHER?

One day, while I was walking down the street to my stepmother's house, a neighbor called out to me. It was Carolyn, the mom of one of my brother's friends. She was also a good friend of my stepmother. She motioned for me to come over to her house. As I approached her, she exclaimed, "I went to school with your mother." I paused, not understanding what she was saying.

I thought to myself, My mother. She continued saying, "Yes, I found your mother's picture in my high school yearbook." We proceeded into the house, where she pulled out the yearbook and showed me my mother's picture. And there it read, Martha Ann Merchant in bold letters. And there was her picture. Carolyn said You look just like your mother. My heart fell to my feet. I thanked Carolyn for telling me. She knew Deanna was my stepmother, and we had never been very close due to the abuse by my father. I walked away from her home, still a bit in shock. WOW, I thought. I did have a REAL Mother.

I had a mother, and she died. For the first time in my life, I pondered MY real mother. I had once belonged. No one outside my family had ever verbalized my mother's existence. I had always felt that I might have hatched from somewhere. I had never known the nurturing love of a mother. For the first moment in my life, I was overwhelmed with happiness that I had a mother, and at the same time, deeply sad that she had died. I had never seen her face, felt her hug.

"I longed for my mother

and grieved her for the first time."

It had only been at my grandparents' house that I had discovered just how much I looked like my mother. I treasured the thought that my mother had always been with me because she had always been a part of who I was, even when I didn't know it.

It was as if my family had shattered into pieces, and no matter how hard I tried, I couldn't put it back together. Just like Humpty Dumpty, all the king's horses and all the king's men couldn't mend what was broken, and neither could I.

CHAPTER 18

CLOSER THAN A FRIEND

By 17 years old, had my own apartment, and bought an old Camaro. I was on a mission, trying to fulfill my promise to God to help others as He had done for me. I started taking others into my little one-bedroom apartment. Bobby's friendship remained a light in a dark time of my life. Sometimes, Bobby would pick me up in his cherry red Chevy Nova. We stopped to get a Dr. Pepper and a Big Red for me; he knew it was my favorite. We would sit in the driveway and talk for hours. He told me he would give me his Chevy Nova, but he had to give it to his little sister.

**"I would share with Bobby deep secrets of my heart.
He always smiled and encouraged me."**

In my heart, it was my destiny to help others who had lost families like mine. It wasn't long before I had an opportunity to help support a family. A young family was being evicted from their apartment. They had two little children. I offered them my bedroom, and I would sleep on the couch until they could get another apartment.

My apartment was always full of people. Bobby would come over, and as we sat on my balcony and talked, he would say. Just say the word, and I'll start throwing all the people over the balcony. He laughed, but he knew my heart was to help someone else, the way God had helped me. After the young couple and their children moved out, I was told about a young girl who had just aged out of foster care. She had left the group home, and her family wouldn't take her in. She needed a place to live. We met, and I offered to let her come live with me. Her name was JoAnn Hoffman. She had lived a rough life, and I knew God wanted me to help her. Maybe we could help each other.

By the end of my junior year, Bobby and Leonard were both seniors and about to graduate. They told me that both their moms wanted them to go to the senior prom. I knew the promise Bobby and I had made to one another about being forever friends. But I had a great love for him and wanted him to have a nice girl. Someone to show him the kindness he had shown me. I suggested that Bobby take JoAnn to the prom, and that I go with Leonard to please their moms. I was still a junior, going to school and working two jobs after school on weekends. JoAnn wasn't working. I bought our prom dresses. We went to Leonard's and Bobby's house for pictures before going to the prom. JoAnn and Bobby hit it off and liked each other. I told her he was very special and to be kind to him. I loved him so much! Bobby was often over at my apartment, but now to see JoAnn. They were an item, and I was happy for them. Although I had known Bobby much longer than JoAnn, they were both my friends.

 I still struggled to do well in school, work two jobs, and overcome my life challenges at the age of 17 years old. It was a challenging time for me, and I didn't have many friends, so Bobby, JoAnn, and Leonard were very special to me!

Months later, after the prom, in October 1979, I was in homemaking class at school when someone ran in and asked, "Hey, did you hear what happened to Bobby?" He got his head cut off. I fell to my feet, screaming and crying. He had been decapitated. They dragged me to the nurse's office, where I kept yelling at the top of my lungs! Not my Bobby, not my Bobby, oh, please God, don't take my Bobby!!! After several hours, the school didn't know what to do with me, so they called an ambulance. The administrators led me to the front of the school building and asked me to enter the ambulance. The last time I saw an ambulance that close was when my mother died. I refused to get inside.

Somehow, I managed to stop screaming and just stood in shock. Someone took me home to my apartment. It was only then that I found out about my friend JoAnn, who had also been murdered that night. They had been at a park together. She was shot in the head.

> *For it is written, he was called the friend of God. (RSV James 2:23)*
>
> *In that moment, God was my friend and my Ever-Present Help in times of great need.*

**"My friends had been murdered.
It was everywhere on the news."**

There had been many decapitations across Houston. I couldn't watch TV for months. I had lost Bobby, the one friend who had been there for me. He always believed in me, and my heart was beyond broken.

As I fell on my knees in the empty funeral parking lot, crying out to God, His Oil of Great Comfort as so many times before, covered me again. Police investigators called me in for questioning. I told them everything I knew about my friend JoAnn and Bobby. Everyone loved Bobby; he had no enemies. They knew everything about me. They said I was a good girl, and they knew I had tried to do better than where I came from to help others. They said a lot of things about my friend JoAnn's background. That she had a rougher life than I knew about. I remembered that she would go with an older man who drove a truck who always bought her new shoes. But I didn't know she had been in prostitution, or I would have helped her. I don't remember speaking to her family, but JoAnn was buried in the prom dress I had bought for her.

I was most sorry that I couldn't help her more. If only, it echoed in my head. If only I had not introduced them. Maybe Bobby and JoAnn would not have been at that park that night. After weeks of investigation, grieving, and overwhelming brokenness, I thought of Bobby, his smile, and, most of all, his special friendship.

It was a loss beyond bearable. I felt alone, and only God's love that you couldn't see was real. I began to believe that; I love you was just words people say. And everyone who says they love you leaves. So much grief, how could anyone process loss beyond measure? Living in survival mode, it seemed like one significant continuous loss. Now I had lost my friend. For this child, all I owned was a heart cry to God. His words are Spirit and Life, and they were all I had to hold on to in those dark days of significant loss and adversity!

Nothing could explain the pain or make it go away. Only His Words of strength and his loving presence of comfort were soothing to my soul. Though God had sustained me during all those years, even early adulthood, I still longed for a family. I longed to belong. I was learning to trust God beyond human reasoning, emotions, or circumstances.

CHAPTER 19

POETRY: MY SHELTER, MY STRENGTH

Writing and drawing were always a great source of healing and finding a place to put the pain. It was like my therapy class. I wrote to try to put the pain somewhere. To put into words the despair of my heart.

"I pray sharing my journey through foster care, brings a better understanding of trauma from being separated from siblings and the loss of family."

Now, I realize the most important message and purpose for writing my story is to help those making critical decisions for children and families in crisis hear the voice of the children they serve. It has always been my heart to grow up to make a difference in the next generation of children in the child welfare system.

Today, my message and mission remain the same. Empowering case workers, teachers, counselors, and judges to better advocate for children in the foster care system.

I wrote and drew a lot during those years. It was the 4th quarter of my junior year, and the school learned I lived on my own, without a guardian or parents. They told me that I was no longer allowed in school because I was only 17 and had no one to authorize my enrollment in school. I was still a ward of the state of California and Texas. I didn't know how to find someone in the government agency to help me enroll in school. Deanna, my stepmom, couldn't or didn't want to help me.

The following year was my senior year of high school. At 18, I was old enough to sign myself into school. I had been in nearly a dozen schools since 8th grade. This was the first time I would get to be in the same school for a second year. This was one of the most challenging times of my life. By the end of the year, I was finally excited to graduate from high school. The school counselor called me into the office to tell me I didn't have enough credits to graduate. It was because I didn't have a guardian to finish the last quarter of my junior year. So I lost all the credits for my junior year.

I was so angry at the system. Specifically, the foster care system kept failing me. It was bad enough that I had no one to help me buy my class ring, class yearbook, or even to help me live. But now, the school system wasn't helping me either!

The counselor calmly said, "The best thing I can recommend is that you get a GED." I ran out of the room, outside to cry out to God, which was my regular go-to in times of crisis. I began to think, if I walked away, then they would win. I will become a statistic that says kids from foster care don't make it! That thought made me even madder and more determined. I told God, please help me not be just a number in a broken system. Please help me make a difference for others.

After my heart-to-heart conversation with God, I went back into the Counselor's office. I sat down and spoke these words boldly and calmly. "Ma'am, I didn't come to this school for a GED; I came for a Diploma, and I am not leaving until you give me one." The counselor responded, Okay, let me get you a half-day schedule for next year as a 5th-year student. God had given me the boldness and confidence I needed! I was now an advocate for myself and one day for thousands of others. The following year, as a 5th-year student, it was still hard to work two jobs and go to high school. But I had learned perseverance and determination. Adversity fueled my determination to overcome.

My father found out I was living in Houston again. He came to see my brothers when I was visiting my stepmother. He told me I would never graduate from high school and never amount to anything. He was angry that he couldn't control me anymore. Of course, his words were hurtful, but I responded to him boldly, saying, "God will never give you another daughter because of the way you treated the one He gave you." Years later, I learned he had another son, Matthew, and I had eight brothers. Still the only girl, which made me even more determined to trust God for a better future. It was the last time I would see him for nearly thirty years.

The following Easter, I got a card from my earthly father, as I called him. My real Father was my Heavenly One, Father God. The words he wrote made me run more into the arms of my loving Father God.

"LOVING YOU MAKES ME SAD AND LONELY.
PERHAPS ONE DAY YOU WILL UNDERSTAND."
DAD (APRIL 26, 1979)

Who would say such a thing to their child? It seemed I could never escape his control and manipulation. Many years later, he came to my stepmom's apartment to try to amend their relationship. I entered the living room, where he was seated in a chair. He immediately told me, just as he had for so many years of my childhood, "I need you to help Daddy. Talk to your brothers so we can be a family again. They will listen to you." I knew my brothers didn't want to talk to him or see him anymore. He reached out and took my hand, pulling me to lean toward him. In that moment,

I felt this strong spirit of manipulation and control that I had felt most of my life. Somehow, God's boldness rose strong in me. I pulled my hand back, and he released his grasp. I boldly said, "Dad, I am not in the fix-it business for you anymore. If you want to have a relationship with your sons, that's between you, them, and God."

And I turned and walked away. I had stood up to my father, and my heart felt free! This feeling of manipulation and control had lost its power.

There is no fear in love; but perfect love casts out fear, because fear involves torment. But he who fears has not been made perfect in love.
1 John 4:18

In that moment, I experienced Faith over Fear. God's Love gave me strength.

I drove away from that apartment that day with a great sense of victory. God had given me the strength to face fear and overcome the insecurities imposed by living in fear of my earthly father's disapproval. Heavenly Father God governs by Faith, not by fear.

In May of 1981, I walked across the stage to graduate and receive my high school diploma from Spring Branch High School. As part of ordering your cap and gown, when you graduate, you receive little thank-you cards to give to parents and relatives who have contributed to your successful graduation. I cried because I didn't have anyone to send one to. My brother John and the mother of a child I babysat were the only two people at my graduation.

I was one of only two of my siblings to graduate from high school. I was told years later that only 10% of youth from foster care graduate high school. And only 1% graduate from college. Years later, I received a bachelor's degree in ministry. By God's strength and transforming pain into purpose, I am part of the 10% and even 1% who succeed beyond foster care.

REBEKAH GRADUATED AS 5TH YEAR STUDENT

My Brothers

I remember all the fun times we had,
and the kicks we got out of just being bad.

Y'all would always think of something fun to do,
and I'd say can I play too?

Y'all would say girls can't play,
but then you'd let me play anyway.

I remember all of our sibling fights,
popcorn and Tarzan movie on Friday nights.

Those good old days have passed away. As I sit here and start
to cry, I don't think I'd trade my brothers, or the good or bad
times for any others.

The Time has Come
The time has come for me to say,
words left unspoken yesterday.

The time has come for me to see,
doors locked behind, have no key.

The time has come for me to look behind,
and gather shattered pieces of my heart, my mind.

Rebekah Mckay, age 17

Will there be enough love to go around?
Do people singing love songs have the right sound?
Will I ever stop being a kid,
and regret all the wrong things I did?

Will the world stop going around when you say stop, cause
God, I really care a lot.

Will the people I love not love me anymore?
Will I be alone like never before?
Will the heart hurt ever go away?
Or will it get worse day by day?

Rebekah McKay, age 14

KEEP TRYING

As I look back and see how well I've done,
I don't have time to stop and cry for battles
that couldn't be won.

I can't ever go back and do the things I didn't get the chance to
do. I can't change all the heartbreak I've been through.

I can't ever forget these things or make them go away,
But I think I should try than go on living in my yesterday.

ONE OF THE LAST PICTURES OF REBEKAH AND HER BROTHERS
JUST BEFORE BEING PLACED IN FOSTER CARE.

CHAPTER 20

COMPLETE SURRENDER
ANSWERED PRAYER

At twenty years old, I was still searching for a place to belong and a family to call my own. A co-worker and friend invited me to go sailing with them, and there I met a man, David, who seemed to love God, and I believed he loved me. All my life, I just wanted to have a family, to really belong. David played the guitar and sang songs to me, which made me feel special. We married only 3 weeks later in a beautiful, small country church. He was a private pilot, and we flew high into the Heavens and life seemed a new and happy adventure. Now I had a husband, and I was full of joy at the prospect of having my very own family.

We were excited to discover after a month of marriage that we would be having a baby! I was overjoyed to finally have my very own family! The joy of the 9 months of carrying my son, planning for his arrival, decorating his baby room! My dream of having a family, to belong to someone, and someone to belong with me. My heart overflowed with joy!

One day, nearly due to give birth, I went to my monthly doctor's visit. The doctor said everything was fine. Over the following weekend, I had a worried feeling inside. I hadn't felt the baby move at all. I would push my stomach at every angle, but still, he didn't move.

I called the doctor's office and explained my concerns, and the phone operator just laughed and said, "Everything is probably fine. We just saw you last week." After insisting, I felt like something was wrong, and the doctor's office agreed for me to come back for a follow-up visit. I walked into the room and lay down on the table. The doctor had the heart monitor around her neck and gently placed it on my stomach. I will never forget that moment of disbelief and gut-wrenching despair when the Doctor uttered the words. "I'm sorry, we can't find the heartbeat." My mind and heart couldn't comprehend the words the doctor spoke.

They said we are sending you for an ultrasound. As I drove to the Ultrasound location, I remembered, just repeating the words. "Please God, don't take my baby". Nine months to the day of our wedding, Jacob David was born on March 20, 1983.

God had been with me in my journey through foster care, child abuse, and being separated from my family. But in this moment, nothing compared to losing my firstborn son. My hope of being the mother, I never had. I felt responsible for being his mommy, and I was supposed to give him life. How could I let my baby die?

Devastation and hopelessness cannot describe what I experienced as I carried him those two weeks, knowing he had no life in his little body. We found out later, after his birth, that the umbilical cord had choked his neck. So tight that it was hard to deliver him.

They said 90% of babies are born wrapped in the umbilical cord in some way. Only one in a thousand dies from it. Instead of welcoming my new

firstborn son home to his beautiful nursery, I had to plan his funeral. I just couldn't.

My mother's sister, Aunt Eleanor, made the arrangements. I was asked to pick out a headstone for my baby. I just couldn't. I could pick out a car seat, clothes, his baby bed, a stroller, but I could not make myself pick out a headstone for my infant son. My grandmother was frustrated with me, and after a year or so, she had a plaque made for my grave. My only consolation was that he was buried next to my mother, Martha Ann.

This time, this pain was beyond what I could bear. I had given God my yesterday, and now He wanted my tomorrow. The tomorrow He had promised to give me. At the age of 21, my times of profound loss had not ended but only begun again. And as I had learned to do for so many years before, I cried out to God in Heaven.

"Oh God, my mother is gone before me,
and now my son is after me.
I am sandwiched between death,
And you are the only one who can save me."

I felt as if I were Abraham, and I carried my only son Jacob in my heart up the mountain to lay him on the altar of great sacrifice. For God, you did not withhold your son from me, and I will not withhold my son from you.

Abba, Father, in your mercy, just as you did for Hannah. She wailed at the altar, and you answered her heart's cry for a son. And I promise, I will take care of all those others who don't have Fathers or mothers and tell them of your Great Love and Tender mercies. I will teach them to run to the secret place, under the shadow of the Almighty—a place of complete surrender.

**"Please God, if you will only give me a second son,
I will name him from your word, raise him in your light,
and give him back to you."**

During this time of great sorrow, I learned that I have always had an altar inside my heart. A place of painful surrender and great love and mercy! Many years later, I drew a picture of what I had felt was the Mercy Seat, the altar in my heart.

And he comforted my heart with a second son, Aaron Daniel. As I had done for my firstborn, I named my second son from my Father's word as a promise to give him back to God. In the Bible, Sarah gave Isaac back to God; I would do the same with His gift of Aaron and all the other children whose lives I would be privileged to touch with the compassion and mercy once shown to me.

Now, I had the son that God had promised, but the husband I had chosen seemed busy in the world and forgot about Aaron and me. Everyone deals with grief differently, and David began to medicate with drugs and alcohol. Once again, I had lost my family and my home. The husband who promised to love me didn't. Aaron was the joy of my life.

"Aaron was my covenant promise
by God Himself to heal my broken heart."

Oh, how I loved my Promised son, Aaron Daniel. He was my special gift of Sunshine during the dark shadows of grief for the loss of Jacob. It was just me, my son, and Jesus.

Rebekah and her second born son, Aaron Daniel

CHAPTER 21

FINDING A FAMILY & FORGIVENESS

I had a good job as a graphic artist and moved into a lovely rental home next door to a man named Stephen. He was kind to Aaron and me. Aaron was only two years old. By the time Aaron was 3 years old, we were married, hoping that this time, I would be truly loved. We bought a beautiful house in the country from God's Country Realty Company. Stephen was a good provider, and he wanted to know God. I thought for the first time in my life that someone would love me and want to keep me. I was grateful and felt God drawing me close. I wanted to say thank you for all He had done for me in my life.

My heart was overwhelmed with gratitude. I cried out to my Father in Heaven. And once again, He was listening. I was invited to a church during a lay renewal weekend. It was about 11:00 pm; I had signed up to pray. It had been years since I had quietly knelt alone in my father's house. The awe of His presence, as I knelt before Him, just as I had done years before as a young girl, I can never forget. On bent knees, I said, "Here I am, Lord; I am ready for you to come into my life again."

It was as if He answered: "Rebekah, I have always been with you and have even brought you here." My life flashed before my eyes, all the nights as a young girl and adult of crying out to Him to save me, the years before, in the girl's home, my foster parents, on the streets, death, shame. Grief and constant loss. I was overwhelmed by the thought: "Oh my God in Heaven, you did save me!" It was truly in God's hands to use me as He chose.

"At that moment, I lay myself on the altar,

the desire of my heart to help the children

who were like me."

After a couple of years of marriage, we signed up to become foster parents. God answered with a little boy named Nathan and a little girl named Natalia. I had taught Aaron that God really listens to children who cry out to Him with a humble heart, and that God would always bless him for sharing his mommy with others who didn't have one.

Many more children came over the next seven years, and my life was so blessed. I began to advocate for children in foster care, speaking at the National Coalition of Foster Care, Child Advocate Inc., CASA National Conference, schools, and at child abuse community awareness events. My heart overflowed with gratitude for God's Faithfulness in my life.

While driving one day, worshipping God to music on the radio, I heard an announcement from Norhill Baptist Church. They were announcing a Forgiveness Seminar coming up in a few weeks. Norhill Baptist was a church in Houston where my family had attended when we were young, many years ago. The leaders all knew my father and some of the situation of what happened to my family.

Although I had forgiven my father in my heart many years ago, I felt compelled to attend. I had not seen my father since I was 17 years old when he had spoken harsh words to me. I went to the Seminar and was moved by its teachings to find my father and tell him in person that I had forgiven him. I asked the leaders if they knew where my father was living. They said the last they heard, he was married to Nellie McKay, preaching at a Methodist Church, and living in Ohio. In the following weeks, I diligently searched online for his contact information. Finally, I found a number listed under his new wife's name. I prayed and then called the number. I asked whether I may speak to Larry McKay. The woman on the other end of the line asked, Who is this? I answered, This is his daughter. The phone immediately went dead. That evening and the next day, I continued to pray for him. That God would allow me to let him know that he was forgiven.

I had no idea how he would respond if I found him. I only knew the Holy Spirit was leading me to see him. It felt like confirmation of the forgiveness I had already given him in my heart. God had shown me that my earthly father could not give me the Godly Love he did not have. And all he had to provide me with was shame, guilt, sorrow, pain, anger, and perversion. But it was not mine to carry. It was my choice to give all my pain to God and not to pass it on to my son, Aaron.

> *having predestined us to adoption as sons by Jesus Christ to Himself, according to the good pleasure of His will, to the praise of the glory of His grace, by which He]made us accepted in the Beloved. Ephesians 1:5-7*
>
> *I knew in that moment, I belonged to Jesus.*

Over the years, each day, month, and year, I learned we were not created to carry the sins of our fathers into the next generation. Letting go of shame, guilt, anger, perversion, and great pain and sorrow, my earthly father had given me was like standing in a pile of rubble in the aftermath of a tornado.

Each day, I would come to the altar to bring God one of my hurts and sorrows, and he would trade me with His Loving Kindness, Tender Mercy, and Unfailing Love. One day, I told God, all I have to give today is rejection. And God gave me Acceptance. His Word reminded me that I had been accepted by my Beloved (Jesus)

The next day, I received a phone call. It was my father, Larry. I told him about God's faithfulness in my life. And how I had overcome great adversity to trust in God by Faith in Jesus. I told him God wanted me to see him. He was pleased to hear from me and sent Aaron, and I plane tickets by the next week to visit him in Ohio. My brother James was a private investigator who had tried to find him for the past 30 years, and God's guidance from the Holy Spirit led him to him in two weeks.

Aaron and I flew to Ohio and met Larry's new family: his wife and her two younger brothers. A youth shut-in was scheduled to be hosted at the church that night. As Aaron went to hang out with the youth and my father was busy coordinating efforts in the gymnasium, I entered the church sanctuary. It was quiet and reverent. I could feel God's Presence and Peace in my heart.

I went up to the pulpit where my father would preach and sat in his big chair behind the pulpit. And I Knew. I just knew judgment and accountability are God's job. It was way too hard and big for the shoulders of a child or an adult.

"I wasn't responsible for my father's failures or even the pain he caused others. God created us to love. And love forgives. "

Today, I am free to love without expectation of anything in return. God had transformed my every sorrow for the benefit of other children, youth, and families. I have been given a mission and a message to tell them they are not created to carry the pain and mistakes of parents and adults in our lives. If we practice this from youth into adulthood, we can overcome anything through Faith.

The next day, we visited my father, Larry's, house and looked at all his books in his giant Biblical library. He began to speak of the past and say he never meant to hurt me. And Deanna, my stepmom, did this or that. I stopped him immediately and said Dad, no matter what, I forgive you. And I'm not here to talk about the past, I'm just here to love you.

The rest of the visit was good. We only stayed three days, which was plenty. I obeyed what God asked me to do. And I left knowing I had confirmation that, just as I had freely received Jesus's forgiveness, I am called to give it away freely.

I remember, over the years following my Forgiveness trip to Ohio, I had enormous Peace and Joy. Each night after I had put our five children to bed, I felt overwhelmingly blessed as I spent time with God, knowing that God could do so much with one life.

Jesus looked at them and said, "With man this is impossible, but with God, all things are possible Matthew 19:26.

I knew in that moment, nothing is Impossible with God.

One night, as I prayed and thought of the hundreds of children God had allowed my life to touch. Kneeling outside on my sidewalk, looking up at Heaven, with a heart overflowing with gratitude, I prayed and thanked God for all He had given me.

This little girl, who cried herself to sleep in a children's home. You have given me a husband who loves me, a big house in the country, filled with children.

**"Who am I, Father God, that you have blessed
me a hundredfold since my childhood?"**

I cried to Him with a humble heart, tears of joy, that He had given me beyond what I could have ever imagined. In that moment, it was as if He said But Rebekah, if it was all gone tomorrow, would you still praise my Name? With weakened knees, I uttered, Father, you know I would. Six months later, after seven years of marriage, my husband left with his secretary. I was in shock. I knew he had become very distant toward me. It was shortly before Christmas last year when my husband informed me that he would be staying in town (Houston) to be closer to the job site.

When he came home on the weekend, I asked him, What's going on with you? How can I help you? He responded that there was nothing wrong. Running out of things to ask, I just wondered if there was someone else. I never expected him to say yes. I said,

What's wrong? You are not that way. He turned and looked directly at me and said, Yes, this is me, and I am that way. The words I had spoken to God reminded me that what was God's to give was really God's all along.

As I fell to the ground in my dirt driveway, I cried out not in despair, but in defiance. "Devil, you have taken my husband, my home, my children, but you cannot claim my soul, because I belong to JESUS!

"For your husband is your Maker, whose name is the Lord of hosts; … God of all the earth. Isaiah 54:5

In that moment, God Himself was a husband to the husbandless.

God has never left me all through my horrific childhood and now even into adulthood. He had always been my ever-present help in times of trouble. And I knew, my Father, Abba, God would rescue me again.

CHAPTER 22

TRUSTING IN HIS LOVE

For the next seven years, I focused on being the best mom I could be to my son, Aaron. He and I were on a journey together, depending on Father God for life and breath. I was a living testimony, learning to live a life of complete surrender of my will to His. During our season of just Aaron and me, God blessed me with a good job in marketing and sales. Aaron never lacked anything. I rented a lovely 3-bedroom home, each of us with our own bedroom and an art room. One day, we were on our way to drop off his clothes at the dry cleaners, and I reminded him that, although he had nice clothes, who he was mattered more than what he wore. He responded, "Mom, I know, but my clothes make me look clean, and I like to keep my reputation clean."

He was my shadow, and he had such a humble heart. While working at Freeman Exhibit Company in sales and marketing, I traveled to Canada, Switzerland, France, and the Netherlands. One of my Oil & Gas clients came from Cochabamba, Bolivia. We talked about the orphanages and the children's significant

137

needs. She invited me to visit and tour the orphanages. So, I prayed and believed we should go. Aaron and I went with two tickets, a massive bag of McDonald's toys that we had collected, and some stuffed animals that we could fit in our luggage. It was a life-changing experience! The world is so big beyond what we can see, ask, or imagine.

Aaron and I spent time together; we called it our special time. We would do art projects, and I even played basketball with him. In those days, autism spectrum was very often misdiagnosed as ADHD,

Behold, children are a heritage from the Lord, The fruit of the womb is a reward.

Psalm 127:3

so Aaron always had difficulty in school and day-to-day activities. One thing he had was a fantastic imagination, and he was so creative, a deep thinker, and loved music!

One day, when he was 13 years old, he came running down the hall saying, "Mom, God is real. He was in the bathroom with me, Mom. I felt Him, his presence filled the whole room, Mom." My son had his own encounter with God and gave his life to Jesus! I did train him up in the ways of the Lord. One day, I wrecked my car and was sobbing uncontrollably. My son Aaron was 13, and he said, "Mom, if Stephen were here, he would be yelling at you, but as the man of the house, I'm not going to do that. Let's pray, Mom." Through my tears, I said, "I can't pray, son, you pray," and together, we knelt beside my bed, and my son prayed for me. Aaron was growing up with a heart for others. I knew the legacy of faith, hope, and love had been passed on to my son. One day, Aaron told me that his best friend, Justin, needed to come live with us. They were more like brothers, having been friends since elementary school. I quickly agreed. By this time, Aaron was 16, and Justin was almost 17. Whenever I introduced Aaron and Justin, I would say This is my son Aaron, and this is my extra-blessing son, Justin.

One day after visiting Jacob's grave at the cemetery, Justin thanked me for taking him into my home and being his other mom. I thought for a moment, then told him, "I am the one who is thankful because I gave my firstborn son to God, not knowing that 17 years later he would give me another son."

"You are my extra blessing, son, Justin. I gave God one son, and now I have three sons: Jacob, Aaron, and Justin."

It was almost exactly seven years since I had laid so many of those I loved on the altar. Aaron was about to graduate from High School, and I felt God's tug on my heart again to touch the lives of hurting children. I told Aaron that I believe God wants me to give away everything I have and help children again. At first, Aaron said, Mom, people don't really do that. But he agreed to pray. Two weeks later, he came to me and said, Mom, I'm ready to give everything away. All I need is my lava lamp and my guitar. Aaron and I prayed. It was then that I was reminded that I must fulfill my promise to God, and He fulfill His promise to me.

"God will use this child's life
to remind Christians that He calls us to reach
out to orphans and restore families."

Aaron and I found him an apartment, and I traded my car to get him a van. Soon afterward, I got a live-in houseparent job at a children's home. The first few days were so tough. The children were so hurt and angry. I felt as if it were me back in a children's home again. This was truly a learning experience. After completing over 60 hours of Boys Town Positive Behavior Intervention training,

It was here that God began to show me how to meet the needs behind the behaviors. In working with such severely traumatized children, I realized that these children needed, wanted, and deserved a family and that institutionalizing them was not the answer.

Every Christian is called to action, to step outside our comfort zone to share His love with others. God is truly a Father to the fatherless, and He works through people, places, and circumstances to accomplish His will.

My life is a testimony to how deep and wide the rivers of God's love flow. We are the vessels He uses to outpour rivers of hope and love into the lives of His children. Each of us must ask ourselves the question. Does his river of love flow through you to touch?

"God didn't just see a little girl with a troubled soul, with a broken family, seemingly abandoned by the world. He saw a testimony to the Power of His love.

He saw in me only our Heavenly Father could: a devoted mother, foster parent, writer, prayer warrior, marketing specialist (marketing the Love of Jesus), gifted artist, and an advocate for abused and neglected children who desperately need to know the love of Jesus. Now I know He really was listening.

God promised never to leave nor forsake us. He has always been with me. And even now, as I advocate for children abroad and in our own communities. As an alumnus of foster care, a foster parent, a house parent, a child and family advocate, and an author, it remains my passion to answer God's call to motivate the body of Christ across our nation as Churches respond in service together to strengthen families and prevent child abuse.

CHAPTER 23

THE 23 GIFTS OF FOSTER CARE

Over the years, I have often been asked about how I overcame childhood trauma and so much adversity in the foster care system. The answer to the question is found in the gifts of moments that have lasted a lifetime, received before, during, and after my journey through foster care. God worked through so many people, places, and circumstances.

"One of the key critical factors in creating success
for youth in and aging out of foster care
is at least one stable, consistent relationship
with a trusted, authoritative figure.
For me, this was always God by Faith in Jesus!"

As caregivers and child advocates, it's important to remember that your influence can only touch the life of a child or youth.

You don't have the power or authority to save or heal all the wounds in the life of a child.

In our lives, we are given much by others on our journey. I was once a child placed from home to home. I have experienced abuse, neglect, and abandonment from those who were supposed to protect me. As I grew up, I began to look at my life and purpose.

Through the years of working through this long grief process of going through old stuff to find something good I could use in my life. I discovered wonderful gifts bestowed upon me by people like you, who gave of themselves. As a child, I began to store away these gifts in a still place in my heart. I have since named this my tool kit for life. Inside, I stored away each gift that has become the tools I need to overcome, persevere, and live.

The true value of each gift seemed to be unknown to the giver. But these gifts given in an unlikely moment, unseen to the naked eye, were the intangibles of the soul. Each has become an intricate part of who I am. Without these gifts, I would only be shattered pieces of myself, trying to succeed in a world without the whole of who I am.

These are the gifts I received, for which there is no price. As children and youth, we cannot identify and thank you for these gifts upon receipt. However, tomorrow was a brighter, better place for this child, and these gifts have multiplied in the lives of others like me simply because you gave a moment's touch that lasts a lifetime.

THE 23 GIFTS OF FOSTER CARE

1. UNCONDITIONAL LOVE

Lots of love gathered along life's way is the bonding stuff that holds the pieces of myself together. It mends the heart and the soul. You can't expect to give me all the love I will need to learn to love myself and others.

"The moment you hug me, I believe I can accomplish a task, or most importantly, show me love in the moment when I am least lovable, I learn that I am worthy of love."

Once I have experienced this thing called unconditional love, I can now identify it on my journey. I now seek it out unconsciously, and I know the value it puts on who I am. On my journey, I learned to gather a little bit of this love wherever I found it along my way. Then I would use it as the glue to put someday the shattered pieces of who I was together again. Loving us when we are difficult will be hard and test you to see if you really mean what you say. But in time, we will know that we are loved, if even for only a moment. And that is not a gift you give, and it fades away. It is the most valuable gift that we take with us when we go.

2. ACCEPTANCE

For all we are and all we are not. If unconditional love is followed by acceptance, I learn that it is okay to be me.

3. OUR FAMILIES

Giving value to our families as they are and as we wish they would be. You can help us find the good in who they are. Maybe we are part of them that is truly good. You give us permission to love and accept them as they are.

4. PAIN AND COMPASSION

Acceptance of our pain may seem strange to most people. Everyone wants to make it all better for us. But if you give us the gift of our pain, we can begin to work through it, to let it go. If you disregard this part of me, I will hold onto it because it is all

I know. I am afraid to abandon so much of this part of who I am. You cannot throw away what is not yours to throw away. God may use it for something good someday. If you let us feel, our pain will lose its power in our lives, and, opposite to what most people think, only then can we begin to heal.

Example: As a foster parent, my 5-year-old little girl began to cry. As I looked over at her, she said, "I miss my mommy." I stopped what I was doing to give her my undivided attention. In that one small moment, I reacted in a way that I knew would help her the most. I didn't say, oh, don't cry, it will be okay. I didn't say, but I love you. I didn't say a word at all. I sat down next to her and, in that moment, felt compassion for her pain and loss.

"I knew there were no words needed.
She needed acceptance of the pain she was feeling.
It was a gift of compassion."

As I sat on the floor beside her, a tear fell from my eye. She immediately stopped crying and said, Mommy, why are you crying? I just looked at her and broke a small smile and said, "I'm sad with you because I know you miss your mommy. I had been her foster mom for over a year before this moment. In this moment, she needed permission, that it's okay for a little girl to miss her mommy.

After that moment, I wondered why I had reacted the way I did. As I thought back on my life, I remembered as a young teenager when I cried while in temporary care with relatives. They thought I was feeling sorry for myself. They never let me be sad about the losses in my life.

Most people just wanted to ignore my sadness or just wanted to fix me. However, later in my life, there would be those who let me be sad and loved me anyway. I discovered this was a gift I had been given and had unconsciously tucked into my toolkit. It had been there all along. I was so blessed and thankful to those who, in a moment of my difficult life, had given me this precious gift, so that, years later, I could give it to another child. Who would have thought a moment's touch could last a lifetime?

5. VALUE OF LIFE

Do you know what it is to have self-worth? What is the value of your life? Imagine you have no worth at all. The greatest gift of ourselves, our belief system. What if there has been no one in your life to validate who you are? Of what value would someone's time be to talk to you, to let you be, to give of their time to you?

Are you worth a moment of time? What if we look around and there are only strangers? What if we feel abandoned and not even worthy of our parents' love? Oh, how will we live without self-worth? What instances can you remember when someone gave a moment in your life to give you self-worth?

6. UNDERSTANDING

Seek first to understand, then to be understood. So often, children and youth in foster care are misunderstood. We are seeking understanding, and most often we can't communicate our needs in appropriate words. It's the adult authorities' job to listen to what we are not saying, but what we would say if only we could say.

7. PATIENCE

We need so much of this one. In your life, what value is patience? We can only learn to use this gift in our lives if someone gives us the chance to try again. Children really do learn what they live and then live what they learn.

8. PARENTS/FAMILY ROLE MODELS

The gift of guidance and love shows us what we may have never seen and may never see again. Even though, as children, my brothers and I slept on a cold, hard floor, there was no place like home. Home was where my brothers were. This becomes the unhealthy picture of what family is. You help us change what we see as usual and give us hope for tomorrow and the family we will create with our children. It is a legacy of change.

Example: My short stay of one summer at the Home of my emergency foster care home. I saw what I might have someday. Children are looking for love and absorb it like a sponge.

"I saw a picture of a family.

A place where you could get mad, be sad,

and they would still love you.

---

9. NURTURING

What if in your life you were never nurtured? Would you be able to nurture your children? It is proven that without touch, children cannot survive. There are too many failure-to-thrive babies who, without your touch of love and nurturing, cannot live. It isn't enough to give life to a newborn. To thrive and grow, an infant must grasp a finger to sit up and learn to walk. Maternal warmth and nurturing teach a child trust. Even if only for a little while, it is worth it. Even though you give nurturing and then have to let go. What if in your life you fell and no one ever helped you up? A child learns trust when they fall on their knees, and you help them get up and put on a Band-Aid.

10. FORGIVENESS

To forgive us teaches for our childish mistakes and defiant behaviors teaches us to forgive others who broke our trust and our hearts.

**"We blame ourselves for everything tragic in our lives
because we only have ourselves to blame.
Help us forgive them so we can begin to release
the pain that is not ours to carry."**

To go through life without the gift of forgiveness is such a heavy burden. Forgiveness teaches us to overcome guilt and find this wonderful place within ourselves and others. It is essential for our lives.

11. POSITIVE DIRECTION

This doesn't sound concise.1but I tell you it is! You help us create a bridge to our future by helping us accept our past. A part of you goes on inside of us. Our minds may forget you, but our hearts never will. There are those who sow the seeds of positive direction in our lives. We reap the rewards later in our lives, when the one who sewed has long since left us; the harvest is Hope.

Example: I believe I was given this gift from many along my journey. A little positive direction here and there has added up in my life, just what I needed to create success for myself and for those whose paths will follow mine.

12. LAUGHTER

What is the value of laughter? Have you ever seen a child angry with the world? You teach us to laugh at ourselves. What is the value of a sense of humor? In your life, how has laughter helped you overcome difficulties? Laughter is good medicine.

Example: I remember that, as a little girl, my gift was a smile; I would smile even when I was sad, and soon I would feel better. Do you smile often? What gift of joy, laughter, and smiles do you give?

13. SONG/MUSIC

You put a song in our hearts to comfort us when we are sad and lonely. We take it with us forever. This has been a comfort to me all my life.

Example: My stepmother took me to see The Sound of Music as a young girl. I remember the song about favorite things, so then you don't feel so bad. This impacted me forever. While in foster care, I would sing to the little ones, and this comforted not only them but me as well. Singing is a joyous thing, a special gift that makes the heart smile.

14. FAITH

Faith teaches us to believe in what we cannot see. By Faith, the love of Jesus is with me wherever I go. Faith teaches me that tomorrow will be better than yesterday, and it is the primary reason I am who I am today. Our faith is our inner ability to sustain life on the inside, while on the outside, our world looks hopeless. By being a living example, you teach us to have faith in Jesus who lives within our hearts so that we might succeed in life.

15. PRAYER

Oh, and please teach us to pray. Even as a child, when I was alone, I would pray, and I knew there was someone listening. It was years later that I traveled to Bolivia and toured several orphanages. As I kneeled before these 30 little girls in a place you would never let your children sleep, I told them the story of how I cried and prayed to God as a little girl at night and that Jesus was listening.

16. IMAGINATION

Hopes, dreams, and wishes are wonderful gifts. I dreamed of how I wished my life would be, and I began to believe it would be someday. Imagine you have no imagination? How could you be empowered to live your dreams? This empowers us to set goals, dreams, and, most of all, hope. Many children and youth in foster care have forgotten how to dream. Maybe it's a game you play to find pictures in the sky. The sky is the limit for what we can do in our lives. I treasure this gift almost more than most.

17. COMFORT

You let us feel maternal warmth and appropriate touch. What if in our lives, no one ever held us when we cried?

18. TEARS

My tears are an expression of my feelings. Please don't take them away from me, for they are not in vain and are of great value on my journey of healing.

19. COURAGE/PERSERVERANCE

We learn we can. What if no one ever read us the story of the little train that could? You teach us to overcome challenges. When the raging waters of life challenge us, they want to drown us in self-pity; courage gives us the wonderful gift of perseverance. I think this gift has become my middle name. Where would I be without this one?

20. HOPE

Such a small word, but what a monumental gift. Most of all, you help us not to be afraid of tomorrow. What if this gift were missing and we never had hope? We are afraid of where we have been, and we do not know where we are going. We are all afraid of what we don't know. Can you recall those times when you felt hopeless to change your circumstances? What did you hope for tomorrow to help you overcome? In what ways have others given you hope in your life?

21. OPPORTUNITY

This gift comes, like most, in everyday moments of life. When you place me in environments and situations that provide opportunities to grow spiritually, physically, and mentally. Then, I learn to create opportunities in my life. I learned to turn crises into opportunities for positive change,

22. INSPIRATION

Who has inspired and mentored you in your life? What value is this gift?

Example: Mr. Brown's art easel. I carried it on the bus and from home to home.

23. LEGACY OF CHANGE

What combination of gifts in the life of one child can do. You will not see today, and you may think you are forgotten. But the gifts you give create a chain of positive changes in many lives. What can one gift do, I ask of you?

Example: As a child in foster care, I soaked up every gift along my journey. The gifts that people like you would give me. When the day came that they were gone, and I had only myself. I discovered they weren't really gone; they were right there with me all along. They had become a part of me.

In summary, you must know that I didn't receive all these gifts in one place. And you will not be the single source in the lives of the children whose lives you only touch. Because of the gift of one touch from those like you in my life, 1 am able to pass this knowledge on to the lives of others, maybe in some small way, yours.

Because someone like you gave love in my life, I have it to give. Maybe just one of your children will go on to carry this legacy and give to others. Maybe just one. I believe it was worth all your tears for one child to have love in their life, from where I stand. I say, I was very much worth it. In the challenging moments, we may only see a child's heart cry in negative behaviors, but God wants us to see what's inside of them.

CHAPTER 24

THE CHURCH IS THE ANSWER

We live in a world of good and evil. The Bible says everything good comes from God. God has given all mankind the freedom of choice. He doesn't force us to choose His law of Faith, Hope, and Love.

Faith is the substance of things hoped for, and the evidence of things not yet seen. No adults in the life of a child have the right to deny children the right to choose to have Faith in Christ Jesus or not. Hope is the one intangible of the heart that every child in foster care needs to survive trauma, neglect, and abuse. Love is the greatest gift, not in words, but in action.

The Church has always been the first responder to care for the hurt and broken among us. Before there was a child welfare system, the Church was created as a place of refuge, faith, hope, and love. It was the centralized hub of the community for town hall meetings, the schoolhouse, and even the hospital.

Many years ago, as a young adult, striving to overcome the trauma of my childhood, I cried out to God again. I told God, "I lost my family, and I want my family back." I heard in my heart, God say, I understand.

I said, Father God, you are GOD, you can do anything. Then I heard these words in my heart that changed everything, and I understood that God understood my pain.

> *He is despised*
> *and rejected by men,*
> *A Man of sorrows*
> *and acquainted*
> *with grief.... Surely*
> *He has borne our*
> *griefs and carried*
> *our sorrows;*
> *Isaiah 53:3-4*

God said, Rebekah, I created the whole world and everything in it for the object of my affection, my very own creation. And then something terrible happened. Sin entered the world, and there came a great gulf of sin, pain, perversion, pride, anger, selfishness, abuse, death, and sorrow. And because I am a Holy God, I was separated from my very own creation, my children.

But then Jesus said, Send me, I will go. And Jesus, the Christ, took off His Crown and Robe of Righteousness and put on the flesh of humanity. He was born of the Virgin Mary and at a set time, laid Himself on the cross, the huge great gulf, to bear the cost of sin and become a bridge, so that I could run across by Faith in Jesus, back into the arms of my Loving Father God.

"And then I heard God say, "Now go tell my church,
I want my family back."

This was confirmation of God's call on my life on my 15th birthday. That He would always be with me as my strength and comforter, so that I could tell others of His Great Love, and that God wants His family back too!

Most large churches today HAVE Social Service outreach ministries, but the grassroots small churches ARE Social Service Ministries! These grassroots small churches are the heart of the community. God has strategically positioned them to serve children and families in crisis in the communities where they live.

There is much data research that shows how connecting children and families to church and faith-based organizations for Spiritual support positively impacts children with trauma.

The local church does more than provide tangible goods and resources, like recovery and transitional housing, food, and clothing. They provide meaning, hope, a sense of purpose, and a strong community support system, fostering resilience and aiding emotional/physical recovery! Although negative spiritual experiences (like questioning God) can occur, practices like prayer, meditation, nature, and connecting with faith communities build inner strength and help process traumatic events, promoting post-traumatic growth.

In Children and Youth Services Review Volume 164, September 2024, 107847, a unique study examined the impact of spiritual and religious strength on behavioral and emotional health among youth in foster care with multiple adverse childhood experiences. Spiritual/Religious Strength (**SRS**) was an overall protective factor of physical and mental wellness, even among traumatized youth.

Belonging to a religious community and having a spiritual belief are protective factors that can support resiliency after trauma. A spiritual belief and/or a positive, affirming religious affiliation can help maintain faith in something greater than oneself and mitigate the overwhelming circumstances that at-risk children have experienced.

Body, Soul and Spirit

Meaning-Making: It helps children find a larger purpose or meaning in their suffering, reducing feelings of helplessness.

Resilience & Coping: Spiritual beliefs act as a buffer, improving emotional regulation and fostering positive coping strategies like prayer or meditation.

Church/Community Support: Belonging to a faith community offers a network of caring individuals, shared values, and a sense of not being alone.

Hope & Connection: Faith in Jesus provides comfort, a sense of safety, and hope for the future, promoting healing.

Prayer & Meditation: Quiet reflection or focused prayer can bring inner peace and spiritual connection.

Community Involvement: Engaging with supportive faith groups fosters a sense of belonging and provides positive role models.

CONCLUSION

Over the years, the only place I found absolute comfort, love and strength was in a Church. When my heart was broken, He bound up my wounds and carried away my sorrows. When I was afraid and almost lost my mind, His perfect Love Cast away all fear and gave me a sound mind. When I was sick, He was my healer. God Himself gave me the Comfort of a Mother! God was a Father to the Fatherless. My refuge and protection. My Savior. My Purpose. My Destiny. Closer than a brother. My Sovereign Hope. My confidence, Life, and breath to my very soul. And called me a friend.

"For so many years, I felt lost in a system
created to protect me but unable to save me.
Because only Jesus could do that."
Now I know, I was not forgotten by God."

Throughout my life, it often seemed that everyone I loved eventually left me, but Jesus never did. Even if He never did another thing for me, I would still choose to serve Him, because He is the only one who never left me.

His love never fails. God didn't just see a little girl with a troubled soul, a broken family, and seemingly abandoned by the world. He saw a testimony to the Power of His Love. He saw an advocate for abused, abandoned, and neglected children, to share His Great love with others!

A child, NOT Abandoned or Forgotten by God.

Journal & Scriptures

The next few pages are some of my confessions of Faith. I would write down and say out loud to myself over and over again.

I pray God's Word will encourage your heart as it has mine. These Journal pages are for your personal notes as you speak God's Word and He hears and answers your Heart cries.

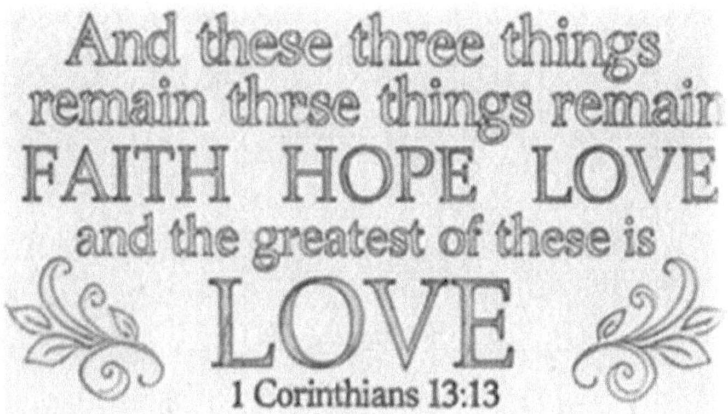

for all have sinned and fall short of the glory of God, and are justified by his grace as a gift, through the redemption that is in Christ Jesus

Romans 3:23-25

For Christ also suffered once for sins, the righteous for the unrighteous that he might bring us to God, being put to death in the flesh but made alive in the spirit,
1 Peter 3:18

According as he hath chosen us in him before the foundation of the world, that we should be holy and Without blame before him in love:
Ephesians 1:4

Can a woman forget her nursing child, and not have compassion on the son of her womb? Surely, they may forget, Yet I will not forget you.[16] See, I have inscribed you on palms of My hands;

Isaiah 49:15-16 (NKJV)

For you created my inmost being you knit me together in my mother's womb. I praise you because I am fearfully and wonderfully made; your works are wonderful; I know that full well.
Psalm 139:13-14 (NIV)

> *He heals the*
> *brokenhearted and*
> *binds up*
> *their wounds.*
> *Psalm 147:3 (NKJV)*

He listens to me every time I call to him.
The LORD protects the helpless; when I was in danger, he saved me.
Be confident, my heart, because the LORD has been good to me.
Psalm 147:3 (NKJV)

He shall cover you with His feathers, and under His wings you shall take refuge; His truth shall be your shield and buckler.

Psalm 91:4

> *For God so loved the world, that He gave His only begotten Son, that whoever believes in Him shall not perish, but have eternal life.*
>
> *John 3:16*

> *He has redeemed my soul from going to the pit, and my life shall see the light.*
> Job 33:28

He who dwells in the secret place of the Most High, Shall abide under the shadow of the Almighty. 4He shall cover you with His feathers, and under His wings you shall take refuge; Psalms 91:1-4

GOD BECAME MY FATHER, AND I BECAME
HIS VERY OWN CHILD

> *Having predestinated us unto the adoption of children by Jesus Christ to himself, according to the good pleasure of his will, (When I lost my family, I cried out to God...and He was listening.) Ephesians 1:5*

A man who has friends must himself be friendly, But there is a friend who sticks closer than a brother.
Proverbs 18:24

And the scripture was fulfilled which says, "Abraham believed God, and it was reckoned to him as righteousness"; and he was called the friend of God.

James 2:23 (RSV)

JESUS SENT HOLY SPIRIT TO BE MY COMFORTER.

Praise be to the God and Father of our Lord Jesus Christ, the Father of compassion and the God of all comfort, who comforts us in all our troubles, so that we can comfort those in any trouble with the comfort we ourselves receive from God
2 Corinthians 1:3-4

I will not leave you as orphans; I will come to you.

John 14:18

A father to the fatherless, a defender of widows, is God in his holy dwelling. 6 God sets the lonely in families, he leads out the prisoners with singing.
Psalm 68:5-6

And now these three remain: faith, hope and love. But the greatest of these is love.

1 Corinthians 13:13

About the Author

Rebekah McKay's experiences as a child in foster care, a foster parent, an adoptive parent, a foster care agency staff, a juvenile probation counselor, and a behavior intervention specialist uniquely qualify her as a child advocate.

She is a volunteer with Christian FAMILY Church graduate of CFCI Bible College with a Bachelor of Ministry Degree. As a dynamic pastor, and speaker, Rebekah educates, equips, and empowers church, community, and state leaders to connect children and families to faith-based resources in their communities.

Rebekah founded Christ Coalition in 2004 in response to the call to strengthen families and prevent child abuse. She is passionate about sharing God's Great Love, bringing families hope, healing, and help to reduce the number of children in foster care.

Join the momentum of Christ Coalition (Churches Have Responded in Service Together), connect to a Faith-based resource, or make a financial contribution at

christcoalition.org or scan the QR code below